make it
SPICY

AMY MACHNAK

photographs by
JOHN LEE

weldon**owen**

CONTENTS

· ·

Turn up the Heat

This is my ideal dinner: I'm sitting at a large table, with friends and family filling every available chair, and the meal lasts for hours. The group is laughing loudly, bringing out more food when we feel the urge, and the aroma of one delicious dish after another fills the air. Someone usually delivers a round of ice-cold beer or maybe a pitcher of margaritas just when it's needed. And at the center of it all, the focus of everyone's attention, are plates of fragrant, spicy, highly flavored foods. Maybe we're exploring authentic Mexican with chipotle pulled beef accompanied with warm tortillas and bowls of jalapeños and cilantro. Or perhaps we're enjoying a platter of Sichuan noodles, a tangle of perfectly cooked wheat noodles dressed with sesame and chile oils, sprinkled with fried peanuts and sliced chiles. If it's Thai we're craving, we're likely spooning ladlefuls of rich and colorful curry over aromatic jasmine rice. Whatever the theme of the feast, the flavors are hot and spicy, and I'm in no rush for the meal to end.

Centuries ago, chiles and spices were carried around the globe by land and sea and introduced to new kitchens. Now, they're found in almost every cuisine in the world, and with good reason: They add flavor, nuance, and, of course, heat and spiciness to foods. But more than that, they add depth and character like no other ingredients can. Think about it: How good are tortilla chips without a fire-roasted salsa in which to dunk them? Would sushi be as delectable without wasabi? And let's be honest, in the absence of the jalapeño, poppers are just cheese sticks.

If you've picked up this book, you most likely have a fondness for hot and spicy foods. So, the next question is this: how hot is too hot? For some people, just a thin slice of serrano chile is enough to make them reach for a glass of water. Other folks are pouring on the hot sauce before the first bite.

Whatever your desired heat preference, chiles and all their heat-toting brethren, like wasabi and mustard, are a great way to add flavor to meals. You can customize the heat level of a dish by starting with a small amount of the spicy ingredient and adding as you go, or by putting sliced chiles, hot-pepper sauce, or chile oil on the table for diners to add as they like. Weeknight dinners are a snap since there's no need for long marinating times when using the instant flavor of spicy ingredients. The Salmon Cakes with Wasabi Mayonnaise on page 22 and the Kimchi Fried Rice on page 87 are two great examples.

Flavor and speed aren't the only benefits of cooking with these hot ingredients, however. Chiles are low in calories and sodium, high in vitamins A and C, and a good source of folic acid, potassium, and vitamin E. Along with spices, they've long been used in Ayurvedic medicine, an ancient Hindu system emphasizing the medicinal properties of foods that is still practiced today as a complement to Western medicine. Capsaicin, a chemical compound naturally present in chiles, is what gives peppers their heat and much of their medicinal value. Today, capsaicin is used in over-the-counter treatments for a variety of medical needs.

No matter how you decide to turn up the heat in your cooking, using chiles and spices is an easy, healthy, and satisfying way to welcome flavor to the dinner table. So try a few recipes that sound exciting in the pages that follow. Get that glass of ice water ready if you think you'll need it, but don't use it as an excuse not to experiment in the kitchen. Above all, enjoy these recipes with as many friends and family you can fit around the table.

A Guide to Heat Levels

The color of a chile has nothing to do with its heat level. In general, color signifies the maturity of the chile, with most specimens green when they are growing, and turning orange, yellow, or red as they ripen. Jalapeños are an excellent illustration of this gradual color change, as they are most commonly harvested and sold when they are green, that is, unripe. But if left to mature on the plant, they will eventually turn red, and occasionally you will see fully ripened jalapeños in the market.

"The larger the pepper, the more mild the heat" has also long been a guideline for selecting chiles. That's because larger ones contain proportionally fewer seeds and membranes, or veins, which are the parts of the pepper that carry some 80 percent of the capsaicin, the source of their incendiary character. But that guideline is often unreliable, as anyone who has bitten into a surprisingly hot poblano chile will confirm. Instead, the best way to judge a chile's heat level is with the Scoville Scale.

In 1912, American chemist Wilbur Scoville developed a method to rate the pungency, or heat, of different chiles. He found that by measuring the amount of capsaicin, he could accurately rate different types of peppers. He then listed the peppers, arranging them from lowest to highest intensity, on a chart, and the Scoville heat unit (SHU) scale was born.

The process Scoville used to determine the heat level is straightforward. The capsaicin in the pepper is extracted and then mixed with a sugar syrup solution. The number of times that the mixture is diluted with the sugar solution until no heat is detected is how the pepper is assigned a rating. For example, the orange habanero chile, which is widely considered one of the hottest peppers commonly available, rates between 150,000 and 325,000 heat units on the scale. This means that it was diluted a minimum of 150,000 times and a maximum of 325,000 times before no trace of heat remained. Alternatively, if you use the same method to test a green bell pepper, the rating on the scale would be zero, as a bell pepper contains no capsaicin. The range between the two numbers can vary greatly due to a few factors, including the conditions under which the chile was cultivated, the variation within a species, and how accurately the test was administered.

But the biggest downfall of the scale is that it relies entirely on perception, that is, how much heat one person can handle. If you've ever shared a plate of nachos with someone, only to see him or her start to sweat while you were wondering why there is so much cheese and so few jalapeños, you understand the problem. Simply put, one person's opinion of hot is not universal.

How to Use This Book

Because the tolerance for chile heat varies so much, this book is designed to be user-friendly for a range of palates. There are three chapters, Mild, Hot, and Fiery, which relate to the lower, middle, and higher ends of the Scoville Scale.

In the Mild chapter, you'll find recipes that have just a touch of heat, which can easily be adjusted higher, lower, or, in some cases, omitted completely. These recipes use milder chiles, such as a single strip of poblano in each quesadilla on page 28, or only a dash of hot-pepper sauce, such as in the filling for Two-Chile Deviled Eggs on page 25.

Recipes in the Hot chapter call for chiles in the middle range of the Scoville Scale, such as the jalapeño and the serrano, and often use a combination of chiles for complexity. These recipes, like Shakshouka on page 62 and Mac 'n' Cheese with Jalapeño Cream on page 67, deliver a bigger kick, but are still usually enjoyed by anyone who is somewhat cautious about eating spicy foods.

The Fiery chapter is for people who like their foods hot and spicy, and that's where you will find the chiles on the upper end of the Scoville Scale, like the Thai chile

and the Scotch bonnet. You'll also find recipes that call for larger quantities of medium-hot chiles, such as the guajillo in the Rack of Lamb with Harissa Crust on page 88.

At the end of the book, you'll find about a dozen recipes, like Pickled Jalapeño Chiles (page 92), Spicy Dijon Mustard (page 92), and Chile-Lemon Oil (page 93), that are great table condiments, sauces, or seasonings for using with dishes in your current repertoire as well as with recipes in the previous chapters. They make good additions to the pantry of any cook who likes to prepare hot and spicy dishes.

Again, all of the recipes in this book can be adjusted to suit your heat and spiciness preference by using a lesser amount of the chile or by removing the seeds and inner membranes (see Working with Chiles, page 12). It's always best to use caution the first time you make a dish. That way, if you discover the result is too mild, you can increase the heat the next you prepare the recipe. That's the beauty of these recipes: the heat level is always adjustable.

Hot & Spicy Ingredients at the Market

There are two main types of chiles, fresh and dried. When shopping for them, you'll need to look for different cues.

CHOOSING FRESH CHILES Look for chiles that have a deep, rich color and are free of bruises, soft spots, and blemishes. The skin should be firm and smooth. If you see wrinkles, the chiles are no longer fresh and their bright, pungent flavor will have begun to turn earthy. Fresh chiles are available at various times of the year, depending on the variety. Once you've brought them home, wrap them in paper towels and store in a sealable container or in the vegetable drawer of the refrigerator. They will keep for up to 1 week.

CHOOSING DRIED CHILES Dried chiles are available year-round. Always try to buy them loose from a bulk bin, rather than in sealed packages. They're generally cheaper, you can inspect them more closely, and you can purchase just the amount you need. Like spices, it's best to buy in smaller amounts and more often, so the chiles don't become stale. Dried chiles should be slightly flexible when bent, rather than so crisp that they snap. Store them in an airtight container in a cool, dry place for no longer than about 3 months or in the freezer for up to 6 months.

CHOOSING OTHER SPICY INGREDIENTS Not all of the spicy heat used in cooking comes from chiles, however. Wasabi, horseradish, and mustard also deliver heat and spice in varying degrees. But because they are not in the same botanical grouping as chiles, they are not given a place on the Scoville Scale. The heat they carry is because of the presence of allyl isothiocyanate, an organic compound that contains sulfur. Its effect is more noticeable in your sinus cavity and lasts for only a few minutes, compared with capsaicin heat, which lands on your tongue and can linger for hours.

Wasabi is available in cans as a powder, which is usually mixed with water to form a paste; in tubes as a paste; and, rarely, in its fresh root form called a rhizome. Store wasabi powder and unopened wasabi paste in a cool, dark cupboard. Once a tube has been opened, it must be refrigerated. If you are lucky enough to find fresh wasabi, rinse it with cool water, wrap in damp paper towels, and refrigerate in the vegetable drawer, changing the towels every couple of days. It should keep for up to 2 weeks.

The recipe for horseradish sauce on page 93 calls for fresh horseradish, which is in season from late fall to early spring. Select firm roots that are free of wrinkles, blemishes, soft spots, and mold. Wrap them in paper towels, slip them into a plastic bag, and store in the refrigerator for up to 3 weeks. Horseradish browns quickly once it has been cut, so be sure to peel and grate it just before serving.

Dry mustard, mustard seeds, and prepared mustard are all called for in this book. Store both dry mustard

(aka powdered mustard) and mustard seeds in tightly capped containers in a cool, dark cupboard for up to 1 year. Once you've opened a jar of prepared mustard, store it in the refrigerator, where it will keep indefinitely.

Working with Chiles

When it's time to use a fresh chile, judge its heat level by cutting off the stem end and very carefully touching the cut side of the slice to the top of your tongue. That simple test will help you decide if you want to reduce the amount, deseed and devein it, or use the amount called for in a recipe.

The only way to lessen the heat of a chile is to remove its seeds and its inner membranes (aka veins or ribs), so if the chile tested too hot for your palate, cut it in half lengthwise. (If you have rubber gloves, you may want to put them on at this point. If you don't have gloves, be careful to touch only the shiny outer side of the chile, not the inside walls, seeds, and membranes.) Now, run the knife along the inside of the chile, keeping the blade parallel to the cutting surface, and carefully remove the seeds and the uppermost layer of textured inner flesh. Discard this part if you know you don't want it. Alternatively, chop it and reserve for any guests who may want to sprinkle a little on top of their food to boost the heat. Keep in mind that this part of the chile is ground zero for spiciness, so even a small amount is highly potent.

Dried chiles are often toasted and/or soaked before using in recipes. Toasting typically involves placing the chiles in a hot, heavy frying pan over medium heat for anywhere from a few seconds to half a minute or so on each side, or until fragrant. Soaking times and water temperatures vary as well, according to both the type of chile and the recipe.

After working with chiles, both fresh and dried, it's imperative that you immediately wash your hands, the knife, and the cutting board thoroughly with hot, soapy water. Avoid touching your eyes, lips, or any other part of your face until you have completed this cleanup.

Seeding a fresh chile (see left)

Roasting and peeling a fresh chile (see page 15)

Seeding and chopping a roasted chile (see page 15)

Ground dried chile, or chile powder, does not present the same danger, though it, as well as dry mustard, wasabi powder, and freshly grated horseradish, can start a sneezing frenzy, so use caution when working with large amounts.

If a recipe directs you to roast, peel, and seed fresh chiles (or bell peppers), such as in the Summer Salad with Chile Vinaigrette (page 18), place the chiles on a grill rack directly over a hot fire in a charcoal or gas grill, on a rack set on a rimmed baking sheet placed under a preheated broiler, or directly over the flame of a burner on a gas stove. Turn the chiles as needed until the skin is blistered and blackened on all sides, 4 to 8 minutes; the timing will depend on the size of the chiles. Transfer the chiles to a bowl and cover with plastic wrap, or to a paper bag and close loosely, and allow to steam until the skins loosen, 5 to 10 minutes. Once they are cool enough to handle, peel away and discard the charred skin using a paper towel. Don't worry if you cannot remove every tiny bit. Slit the chile lengthwise, open it up, and, using a small spoon or the tip of a knife, scoop out and discard the seeds and membrane, then cut away the stem. The chile is now ready to use as directed in the recipe. (See tip at right on stocking your freezer with roasted chiles.)

Stocking a Hot & Spicy Pantry

Preparing hot and spicy dishes is easy to do any time the mood strikes if you stock your pantry wisely. Items like hot-pepper sauces, chile pastes, and chile oils keep well in the refrigerator for months, and prepared mustards—whole grain, smooth, brown (deli style), yellow, Dijon, and more—will keep indefinitely. Store an assortment of dried chiles in a cupboard, and outfit your spice cabinet with red pepper flakes, dry mustard, mustard seeds, and wasabi powder. With basics like these on hand, a few fresh accents like herbs, ginger, or garlic are all you need to get started in the kitchen.

Hot & Spicy Tips & Tricks

- When prepping chiles on the higher end of the Scoville Scale, wear rubber gloves to protect your skin.

- For the spiciest dishes, leave the seeds and membranes intact in chiles. For a milder flavor, remove and discard the seeds and membranes, or save them to chop and use as a potent garnish.

- Wash your hands, the cutting board, and the knife well after working with fresh chiles or rehydrated dried chiles. Avoid touching your face, eyes, or other sensitive areas until you're sure you've washed away every trace of capsaicin.

- Roast, peel, and seed extra chiles when you are preparing roasted chiles for a recipe. Freeze the extras in an airtight container for up to 6 months to use whenever you're short on time and need roasted chiles for a dish.

- Keep your pantry stocked with hot-pepper sauces, chile pastes, mustards, and other spicy seasonings so that a spicy meal is always possible, even on short notice. Be sure to rotate out old spices and dried chiles twice a year to avoid using stale ingredients.

- If a chile-laden dish sets your mouth on fire, eat some bread or a mouthful of plain rice or drink some milk to quell the flames. Although a beer may sound better, starches and dairy products are more effective weapons against the heat.

- When using fresh chiles in recipes that will sit for a while before being eaten, such as salsa, know that the heat will intensify and spread throughout as time goes by. If you're prepping ahead, start with the smaller amount of chile and add more just before serving, after you've tasted the dish.

- If a recipe calls for dried spices and chiles, toasting them slightly in a dry pan before using (like in the Shakshouka on page 62) helps to bloom the flavor.

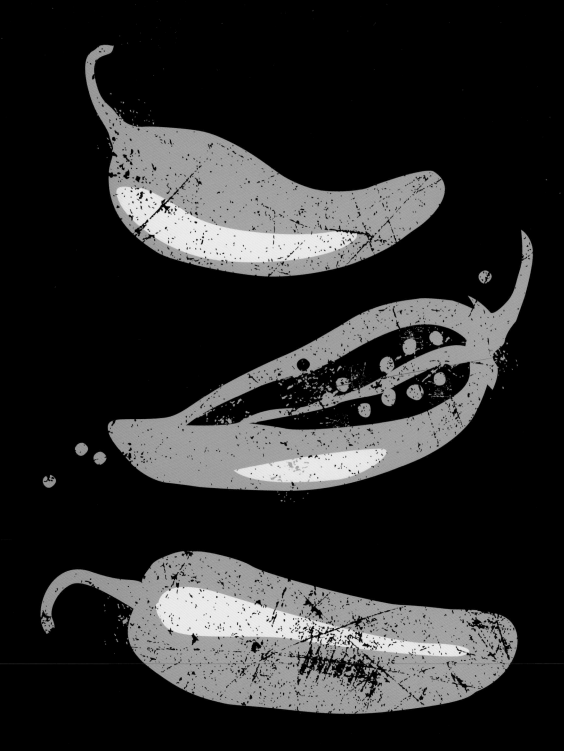

MILD

18 Summer Salad with Chile Vinaigrette **21** Spicy Red Shrimp
22 Salmon Cakes with Wasabi Mayonnaise **25** Two-Chile Deviled Eggs
26 Nachos with Two Cheeses **28** Quesadillas with Poblano Chiles
29 Bucatini with Arrabbiata Sauce **31** Thai-Style Chicken with
Lemongrass **32** Spicy Seafood & Sausage Gumbo
34 Whole Snapper with Creole Spices
35 Red Curry Beef with Thai Spices **37** Turkey Enchiladas
with Red Chile Sauce **38** Pulled Beef Tacos
40 Mashed Potatoes with Wasabi & Green Onion
41 Cauliflower Gratin with Red Pepper & Capers

IN THIS RECIPE, PEAK-OF-THE-SEASON TOMATOES ARE DRESSED IN A MILD POBLANO CHILE VINAIGRETTE. OCCASIONALLY A HOT CHILE TURNS UP, SO TASTE YOUR BATCH BEFORE ALL OF THEM GO INTO THIS VINAIGRETTE.

SERVES
4–6

SUMMER SALAD
WITH CHILE VINAIGRETTE

3 large poblano chiles

2 small garlic cloves, unpeeled

1 tbsp apple cider vinegar

Pinch of sugar

¾–1 cup (6–8 fl oz/180–250 ml) olive oil

Kosher salt and freshly ground pepper

3 lb (1.5 kg) tomatoes, in a mixture of shapes, sizes, and colors, cored and sliced

2 avocados, pitted, peeled, and sliced lengthwise

2 tbsp chopped fresh chives

12 large fresh basil leaves, finely sliced

1 Roast, peel, and seed the chiles as directed on page 15. Set aside.

2 In a small, dry frying pan, toast the garlic cloves over medium heat, turning them often, until they soften and their skins blacken, 8–10 minutes. Let the cloves cool, then peel.

3 In a blender, whirl the chiles, garlic, vinegar, and sugar until smooth, adding a little water (about 1 tbsp at a time) if needed to blend. With the motor running, slowly add as much of the oil as needed to create a vinaigrette with the consistency of heavy cream. If it is too thick, add a little water. Taste and season with salt and pepper.

4 Arrange the tomatoes and avocado slices on individual salad plates and drizzle each serving with the vinaigrette. Sprinkle with the chives and basil and serve.

SPICY RED SHRIMP

1 lb (500 g) jumbo or large shrimp

1 tbsp minced garlic

1 tbsp grated fresh ginger

2 tsp cayenne pepper

1 tsp freshly ground black pepper

1 tsp ground cumin

½ tsp ground cinnamon

¼ tsp ground cloves

¼ tsp ground turmeric

2 tbsp gin

1 tsp firmly packed dark brown sugar

2 tbsp mustard oil or olive oil

1 tbsp fresh lemon juice

Chopped fresh cilantro (optional)

1 Peel the shrimp, with the tail segments intact, then devein them and place in a shallow dish. In a small bowl, combine the garlic, ginger, cayenne, black pepper, cumin, cinnamon, cloves, turmeric, gin, and brown sugar and mix well to form a paste. Rub the paste evenly over the shrimp. Let sit at room temperature for about 30 minutes.

2 In a large frying pan, warm the oil over high heat. When the oil is very hot, add the shrimp and cook, tossing, until they turn pink and opaque, about 5 minutes.

3 Remove from the heat, sprinkle with the lemon juice and cilantro (if using), transfer to a serving dish, and serve.

RUBBED WITH A SPICE PASTE PRIZED BY GOAN COOKS, THESE SHRIMP PAIR WELL WITH A GREEN SALAD AND A PITCHER OF YOUR FAVORITE ICE-COLD TROPICAL FRUIT JUICE.

SERVES
2–4

WASABI IS THE
JAPANESE VERSION OF
HORSERADISH AND IS
INTENSELY POTENT IN
EVEN THE SMALLEST
OF DOSES. IF YOU'RE
LUCKY ENOUGH TO
LOCATE THE FRESH
ROOT FROM AN ASIAN
MARKET, START WITH
ONLY A FEW GRATES
AND ADD TO TASTE
AS YOU GO.

SERVES
3-6

SALMON CAKES
WITH WASABI MAYONNAISE

½ lb (250 g) cooked salmon fillet

1 tbsp minced white onion

1 cup (1½ oz/45 g) panko bread crumbs

Kosher salt and freshly ground pepper

½ cup (4 fl oz/125 ml) mayonnaise, plus about 1 tbsp

1 tsp wasabi paste or powder

½ tsp honey

1 tsp fresh lemon juice

Canola oil for frying

¼ cup (1½ oz/45 g) all-purpose flour

1 large egg, lightly beaten

2 tbsp chopped fresh chives

1 Flake the salmon into a bowl, removing any errant bones. Add the onion, half of the bread crumbs, ¼ tsp salt, a few grinds of pepper, and 1 tbsp of the mayonnaise and mix gently. Add more mayonnaise if needed to bind.

2 Divide the mixture into 6 equal portions and form each portion into a cake about 3 inches (7.5 cm) in diameter. Place on a plate, cover, and refrigerate for about 15 minutes to firm up and to blend the flavors.

3 Meanwhile, in a bowl, whisk together the remaining ½ cup (4 fl oz/125 ml) mayonnaise with the wasabi, honey, and lemon juice. Taste and adjust the seasoning if needed.

4 Pour the oil to a depth of ½ inch (12 mm) into a large, heavy frying pan and place over medium heat. While the oil is heating, put the flour, egg, and the remaining bread crumbs in 3 separate bowls. Working with one salmon cake at a time, evenly coat with the flour, shaking off the excess; then with the egg, allowing the excess to drip off; and finally with the bread crumbs, again shaking off the excess. Set the coated cakes on a clean plate as you work.

5 Once the oil is shimmering, carefully add the cakes to the hot oil and fry, turning once, until golden brown on both sides, about 2 minutes on each side. Serve each cake with a dollop of wasabi mayonnaise, sprinkle with some chives, and serve.

TWO-CHILE DEVILED EGGS

6 large eggs

1 green onion, minced

1½ tsp hot-pepper sauce

1 tsp grated lemon zest

3 tbsp mayonnaise

Kosher salt and freshly ground pepper

Pickled Jalapeño Chiles (page 92)

1 In a saucepan, combine the eggs with cold water to cover by at least 1 inch (2.5 cm), place over medium heat, and bring to a boil. When the water reaches a full boil, immediately remove the pan from the heat, cover, and let sit for 15 minutes.

2 Uncover the pan and drain the eggs. Place the eggs under cold running water until the eggs are cool. Drain the eggs again, peel, and cut in half lengthwise. Using the tip of a spoon, carefully dislodge the yolks and put them in a bowl. Set the whites aside, hollow side up.

3 Mash the yolks with a fork until very smooth. Add the green onion, hot sauce, lemon zest, and mayonnaise and mix well with the fork. The mixture should have a smooth, creamy consistency. Season with salt.

4 Using a small spoon, divide the egg yolk mixture evenly among the egg whites, mounding the mixture slightly in the center. Garnish each egg with some black pepper and a jalapeño slice. Arrange on a serving platter and serve.

TOPPING EACH EGG WITH A THIN SLICE OF HOMEMADE PICKLED JALAPEÑO DOUBLES DOWN ON THE DEVILISH NATURE OF THESE APPETIZERS.

SERVES
4–6

NOT ALL PEPPER
JACK CHEESES
ARE CREATED EQUAL
IN HEAT RATIO,
WITH SOME BRANDS
USING CHILES HIGHER
ON THE SCOVILLE
SCALE THAN OTHERS.
IF YOU NEED TO
TAME THE HEAT,
SUBSTITUTE A BIT OF
REGULAR MONTEREY
JACK INSTEAD.

SERVES
4–6

NACHOS
WITH TWO CHEESES

1 bag (9 oz/280 g) tortilla chips

1 large white onion, chopped

¾ lb (375 g) pepper jack cheese, shredded

2 oz (60 g) Cotija cheese, crumbled

Pickled Jalapeño Chiles (page 92)

Chopped fresh cilantro

Cubed avocado

Roasted Habanero Chile & Tomato Salsa (page 91)

Sour cream

1 Preheat the broiler. Layer half of the tortilla chips in a shallow ovenproof frying pan or on a rimmed baking sheet. Scatter half each of the onion and of the pepper jack and Cotija cheeses over the chips. Scatter the remaining chips over the onion and cheese layer, then top with the remaining onion and cheeses.

2 Place under the broiler and cook until the cheeses are melted, 3–8 minutes, depending on the distance from the heat source. Watch closely, as the cheeses will burn easily.

3 Remove from the oven, let cool slightly, and then sprinkle the jalapeño slices, cilantro, and avocado cubes. Add small dollops of the salsa and sour cream over the top, and serve.

THESE QUESADILLAS GO GOURMET THANKS TO THE ADDITION OF FRESH EPAZOTE, A WILD AND PUNGENT HERB THAT CAN BE FOUND IN LATIN MARKETS. IF YOU CAN'T LOCATE FRESH, A SPRINKLE OF THE DRIED HERB WILL ALSO BE DELICIOUS.

SERVES
6

QUESADILLAS
WITH POBLANO CHILES

2 poblano chiles

12 white corn tortillas

½ lb (250 g) Muenster or Monterey jack cheese, shredded

12 fresh epazote leaves (optional)

1 white onion, thinly sliced

Canola or safflower oil for frying

Guacamole

Salsa Fresca (page 90) or Salsa Verde (page 90)

1 Roast, peel, and seed the chiles as directed on page 15, then cut each chile lengthwise into 6 strips each ¼ inch (6 mm) wide. Place a tortilla on a clean work surface. Place about 2½ tbsp of the cheese on half of the tortilla, leaving a border of about ½ inch (12 mm) uncovered. Top with 1 epazote leaf (if using), 1 chile strip, and some onion. Fold the tortilla in half and press the edges together with your fingertips. Set aside, covered with a barely dampened towel. Repeat until all the quesadillas are made.

2 Preheat the oven to 200°F (95°C). Line a large baking sheet with paper towels.

3 In a large frying pan, warm 2 tbsp oil over high heat. When the oil is shimmering, fry the quesadillas, one at a time, until golden, 1–2 minutes on each side, replenishing the oil as necessary. Using a spatula, transfer to the towel-lined pan to absorb any excess oil, then transfer to a heatproof platter and keep warm in the oven. When all of the quesadillas are ready, serve, accompanied with the guacamole and salsa.

BUCATINI
WITH ARRABBIATA SAUCE

¼ cup (2 fl oz/60 ml) olive oil

2 garlic cloves, minced

1 tsp red pepper flakes

1 can (28 oz/875 g) Italian-style
whole tomatoes, preferably
San Marzano, drained and chopped

Kosher salt

1 lb (500 g) dried bucatini

1 In a large nonreactive frying pan, warm the oil over medium heat. Add the garlic and red pepper flakes and cook, stirring, until the garlic is lightly golden, about 2 minutes. Add the tomatoes and 1 tsp salt, stir well, and bring to a simmer. Reduce the heat to low and cook, stirring occasionally, until the sauce is thickened, about 20 minutes.

2 About 10 minutes before the sauce is ready, bring a large pot of salted water to a boil over high heat. Add the pasta, stir well, and cook until al dente, according to the package directions. Reserve about 1 cup (8 fl oz/250 ml) of the cooking water. Drain the pasta.

3 With the sauce still over low heat, transfer the pasta to the pan with the sauce and stir well. Adjust the consistency of the sauce with some of the reserved cooking water if needed. Transfer to a serving bowl or individual plates and serve.

IN ITALIAN,
ARRABBIATA MEANS
"ANGRY" AND REFERS
TO THE RED PEPPER
FLAKES ADDED TO
SPICE UP THE SIMPLE
TOMATO SAUCE THAT
IS TOSSED WITH
THE PASTA.

SERVES
4–6

THAI-STYLE CHICKEN
WITH LEMONGRASS

½ cup (2 oz/60 g) minced lemongrass, tender bottom part only

3 tbsp grated fresh ginger

3 tbsp fish sauce

Grated zest of 1 lime

3 tbsp fresh lime juice

3 garlic cloves, coarsely chopped

1 tsp red pepper flakes

4 skin-on, bone-in chicken breasts, about ¾ lb (375 g) each

2 limes, halved crosswise

Hot cooked rice

Chopped fresh cilantro

1 In a blender, combine the lemongrass, ginger, fish sauce, lime zest, lime juice, garlic, red pepper flakes, and 2–3 tbsp water and whirl until a thick paste forms. Spread the lemongrass mixture evenly over both sides of each chicken breast, place in a shallow dish, cover with plastic wrap, and refrigerate for at least 1 hour or for up to 4 hours.

2 Prepare a charcoal or gas grill for indirect medium heat by either building the coals to one side of the charcoal grill or turning half the burners off on a gas grill.

3 Oil the grill grates. Place the chicken, skin side down, on the grill rack over the unheated area. Cook, covered, turning it over after 15 minutes, until no pink is visible when a breast is cut into at the thickest part near the bone, about 35 minutes. In the last few minutes, grill the lime halves, cut side down, until grill marks appear.

4 Transfer the chicken to individual plates and serve with rice, cilantro, and grilled limes.

LEMONGRASS, WHICH ADDS A FRAGRANT LEMON SCENT TO THIS DISH, CAN BE FOUND IN THE PRODUCE SECTION OF WELL-STOCKED GROCERY STORES. EXTRA STALKS CAN BE STORED IN THE FREEZER FOR UP TO 3 MONTHS.

SERVES
4

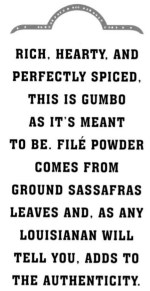

RICH, HEARTY, AND
PERFECTLY SPICED,
THIS IS GUMBO
AS IT'S MEANT
TO BE. FILÉ POWDER
COMES FROM
GROUND SASSAFRAS
LEAVES AND, AS ANY
LOUISIANAN WILL
TELL YOU, ADDS TO
THE AUTHENTICITY.

SERVES
6

SPICY SEAFOOD & SAUSAGE GUMBO

½ lb (250 g) okra

½ cup (4 fl oz/125 ml) canola oil

6 tbsp (2 oz/60 g) all-purpose flour

1 large yellow onion, diced

1 *each* red and green bell pepper, seeded and diced

3 garlic cloves, minced

5 cups (40 fl oz/1.25 l) fish stock

1 can (14½ oz/455 g) diced tomatoes, with juice

2 bay leaves

2½ tbsp Creole seasoning blend

Kosher salt and freshly ground pepper

½ lb (250 g) andouille sausage, sliced on the diagonal

1 lb (500 g) large shrimp, peeled, deveined, and tails intact

6 oz (185 g) lump crabmeat

1 tsp filé powder

Hot cooked rice

2 tbsp minced fresh flat-leaf parsley

1 Trim the stems from the okra pods, then cut the pods crosswise into slices ½ inch (12 mm) thick.

2 In a large, heavy pot, warm 2 tbsp of the oil over medium heat. Add the okra and cook, stirring occasionally, until golden brown and softened, about 15 minutes. Transfer to a bowl and set aside.

3 In the same pot, warm the remaining 6 tbsp (3 fl oz/90 ml) oil over medium heat for 2 minutes. Whisk in the flour to form a roux, then cook, stirring constantly with a wooden spoon, until dark brown, about 4 minutes. Add the onion and bell peppers and cook, stirring occasionally, until softened, 8–10 minutes. Add the garlic and cook for 1 minute longer. Add the reserved okra, stock, tomatoes and juice, bay leaves, and Creole seasoning, and season with salt and pepper. Raise the heat to medium-high and bring to a boil, then reduce the heat to medium-low and simmer for 30 minutes to blend the flavors.

4 Stir in the sausage, shrimp, and crabmeat, and cook until the sausage is heated through and the shrimp are pink, about 3 minutes longer. Stir in the filé powder. Remove from the heat and remove and discard the bay leaves. To serve, spoon the rice into bowls, ladle the gumbo on top, and garnish with the parsley.

GRILLING A WHOLE
FISH STUFFED WITH
ROBUST SPICES AND
ANDOUILLE SAUSAGE
IS AN EASY AND
FLAVORFUL WAY TO
COOK SEAFOOD FOR
A SMALL GROUP.

SERVES
4

WHOLE SNAPPER
WITH CREOLE SPICES

¼ cup (1 oz/30 g) hot paprika

3 tbsp granulated garlic

1½ tbsp granulated onion

1½ tbsp cayenne pepper

1 tbsp *each* dried oregano and thyme

1½ tsp smoked paprika

Kosher salt and freshly ground black pepper

2 whole red snappers, 2½–3 lb (1.25–1.5 kg) each, cleaned, with head and tail intact

2 andouille sausages, sliced on the diagonal about ¼ inch (6 mm) thick

4 green onions, cut into 2-inch (5-cm) pieces

2 tbsp mayonnaise

1 To make the spice rub, mix the hot paprika, granulated garlic and onion, cayenne, oregano, thyme, smoked paprika, 3 tbsp salt, and 2½ tbsp black pepper. You should have about ⅔ cup (4½ oz/140 g). You will need only 2–3 tbsp for this recipe. Store the remainder covered tightly in a cool, dark place for up to 1 month.

2 Prepare a charcoal or gas grill for indirect medium heat by either building the coals to one side of the charcoal grill or turning half the burners off on a gas grill.

3 Season the fish generously inside and out with the spice rub. Divide the sausage and green onions between the fish cavities and secure them closed with a toothpick or kitchen string. Brush 1 tbsp of the mayonnaise on each fish, coating both sides evenly.

4 Oil the grill grates. Place the fish on the grill rack over the unheated area. Cook, covered, using 2 large spatulas to turn the fish after 8–10 minutes, for 15–20 minutes total. To test for doneness, slide a paring knife into the thickest part of the flesh near the bone, pull it out, and touch it to your wrist. If it is warm, the fish is ready. Check the fish often toward the end of the cooking time.

5 Using the spatulas, transfer the fish to a large platter and let rest for about 5 minutes. One at a time, carefully lift the top fillet from each fish, then lift away and discard the central bone, and serve.

RED CURRY BEEF
WITH THAI SPICES

1 lb (500 g) beef tenderloin

¼ cup (2 fl oz/60 ml) fish sauce

1½ tbsp firmly packed brown sugar

1 tsp tamarind paste (optional)

1 tsp fresh lime juice

2 tbsp canola oil

1 small yellow onion, halved and thinly sliced

1 small red bell pepper, seeded and thinly sliced

1 cup (8 fl oz/250 ml) coconut milk

2 tbsp Thai red curry paste

1 tbsp chopped dry-roasted peanuts

8–10 fresh Thai or sweet basil leaves

Hot cooked rice

1 Put the beef in the freezer for 30 minutes to firm up, then cut against the grain into slices about ⅛ inch (3 mm) thick. Set aside.

2 In a small bowl, stir together the fish sauce, brown sugar, tamarind paste (if using), and lime juice. Set aside.

3 In a Dutch oven or large, heavy pot, warm the oil over high heat. Add the onion and bell pepper and cook, stirring, until just tender, about 5 minutes. Add the coconut milk and heat just until it begins to bubble. Stir in the curry paste, bring to a simmer, and cook, stirring occasionally, for about 5 minutes. Add the reserved fish sauce mixture and simmer until the curry thickens, 7–10 minutes. Reduce the heat to low, add the beef slices, and simmer until the beef is almost cooked through but still pink in the center, 5–7 minutes longer.

4 Transfer the curry to a bowl, garnish with the peanuts and basil, and serve, accompanied with the rice.

ALTHOUGH SOME THAI CHEFS WHIP UP PUNGENT, SPICY CURRY PASTES IN A RAINBOW OF COLORS, YOU CAN BUY THESE BOLD SEASONINGS AT MOST WELL-STOCKED GROCERY STORES.

SERVES
4–6

TURKEY ENCHILADAS
WITH RED CHILE SAUCE

10 ancho chiles, stemmed, seeded, and torn into pieces

1 can (14½ oz/455 g) diced tomatoes, with juice

½ white onion, coarsely chopped, plus 1 small white onion, thinly sliced and separated into rings

6 garlic cloves, chopped

1 tsp dried Mexican oregano

1½ cups (12 fl oz/375 ml) chicken broth

4 tbsp (2 fl oz/60 ml) canola oil

Kosher salt

12 (6-inch/15-cm) white corn tortillas

About 2 cups (12 oz/375 g) coarsely shredded cooked turkey

½ cup (4 oz/125 g) sour cream

6 radishes, thinly sliced

1 Put the chiles in a heatproof bowl, add boiling water to cover, and let soak until soft, about 15 minutes, then drain. In a blender, whirl the chiles, tomatoes and juice, chopped onion, garlic, and oregano until blended, adding broth as needed to achieve a smooth consistency.

2 Preheat the oven to 325°F (165°C). In a frying pan, warm 1 tbsp of the oil over medium heat. Pour in the chile mixture and cook, stirring, until thick, about 2 minutes. Add the remaining broth and cook, stirring, until thick, about 5 minutes. Season with salt. Spoon a thin layer of the sauce into 1 or 2 shallow baking dishes.

3 In another frying pan, heat the remaining 3 tbsp oil over medium heat until sizzling hot. Using tongs, quickly drag the tortillas, one at a time, through the oil to soften them, then pat dry with paper towels. Dip a tortilla into the sauce in the frying pan and lay it on a plate. Spread a heaping 1½ tbsp of the turkey near the edge of the tortilla, roll up the tortilla, and place, seam side down, in the prepared dish with the sauce. Repeat with the remaining tortillas and turkey, arranging the enchiladas side by side. Spoon the remaining sauce evenly over the top.

4 Bake the enchiladas until heated through, about 15 minutes. Top with the sour cream, onion rings, and radishes and serve.

THE ANCHO CHILE HAS A BITTERSWEET CHOCOLATY FLAVOR AND MILD HEAT SO THE LARGE QUANTITY CALLED FOR HERE WON'T SET YOUR PALATE ABLAZE.

SERVES
6

THE CHIPOTLE
SALSA THAT COATS
THESE BEEF TACOS
OFFERS THE PERFECT
AMOUNT OF HEAT. THE
SALSA NATURALLY
SEPARATES, SO IF YOU
PREFER A CREAMIER
CONSISTENCY, PULSE
IT IN THE BLENDER.

SERVES
6–8

PULLED BEEF TACOS

3 tbsp plus ⅓ cup (3 fl oz/80 ml) olive oil

1½–2 lb (750 g–1 kg) beef chuck roast

Kosher salt and freshly ground pepper

1 white onion, quartered

1 head garlic, halved crosswise

¼ cup (2 oz/60 g) chopped chipotle chiles in adobo sauce

3 tbsp apple cider vinegar

3 garlic cloves, minced

Pinch of sugar

2 avocados, pitted, peeled, and sliced

2 tomatoes, diced

1 small red onion, diced

3 large radishes, cut into wedges

1 jalapeño chile, sliced

⅓ cup (½ oz/15 g) coarsely chopped fresh cilantro

2 cups (4 oz/125 g) finely sliced romaine lettuce

24 corn tortillas, heated

1 Preheat the oven to 275°F (135°C). In a heavy-bottomed pot or Dutch oven, heat 3 tbsp of the oil over medium heat until hot. Season the roast generously with salt and pepper. Cook the roast, turning as needed, so it's browned on all sides, about 10 minutes total. Add the onion, halved garlic, and just enough water to come halfway up the sides of the roast; do not submerge with liquid. Cover the pot and place in the oven. Cook until the roast is tender and splits easily when pulled on with a fork, about 2 hours. Let the roast cool in the broth, then pull the roast into large pieces. Rewarm the roast in a little of the broth to serve or refrigerate in broth for up to 2 days.

2 Meanwhile, in a bowl, whisk together the chipotle chiles, vinegar, minced garlic, sugar, and ½ tsp salt until blended. Add the remaining ⅓ cup (3 fl oz/80 ml) oil, whisking just to blend. Season with more salt to taste. Let the mixture sit to develop flavor. The sauce can be refrigerated for up to 2 days.

3 Assemble all the topping ingredients in individual bowls. Set out with the warmed roast and tortillas so guests can assemble their own tacos.

MASHED POTATOES
WITH WASABI & GREEN ONION

3½ lb (1.75 kg) russet potatoes, peeled and quartered

Kosher salt and freshly ground pepper

4 tbsp (2 oz/60 g) unsalted butter

½ cup (4 fl oz/125 ml) heavy cream

½ cup (4 fl oz/125 ml) whole milk

2–3 tsp wasabi paste or powder

¼ cup (¾ oz/20 g) minced green onion

1 In a large saucepan, combine the potatoes, a large pinch of salt, and enough cold water to cover generously. Bring to a boil over high heat, reduce the heat to low, and cook, uncovered, until the potatoes are tender but not falling apart when pierced with a knife, 20–30 minutes. Drain the potatoes and return them to the hot pan. Place over medium heat for 1–2 minutes to eliminate any remaining moisture.

2 Meanwhile, in a small saucepan, combine the butter, cream, and milk and warm over medium-low heat, stirring to melt the butter. Add 2 tsp of the wasabi paste and a pinch each of salt and pepper and stir to combine. Taste and adjust the seasoning with salt, pepper, and the remaining 1 tsp wasabi paste if desired. Remove from the heat and keep hot.

3 Transfer the potatoes to a stand mixer fitted with the paddle attachment and mix on low speed until they break up, then gradually increase the speed to medium. When the potatoes are almost smooth, turn off the mixer and add half of the warm cream mixture. On medium speed, mix to combine, adding more of the cream mixture as needed to reach a creamy consistency; do not overmix the potatoes or they will become gluey. Stir in the green onion, season with salt and pepper, transfer to a serving dish, and serve.

CAULIFLOWER GRATIN
WITH RED PEPPER & CAPERS

1 tbsp plus 1 tsp unsalted butter, plus butter for the baking dish

1 head cauliflower, trimmed

3½ tbsp all-purpose flour

1½ cups (12 fl oz/375 ml) whole milk

Kosher salt and freshly ground black pepper

⅓ cup (⅔ oz/20 g) fresh bread crumbs

1 tbsp capers, rinsed and drained

1 tsp red pepper flakes

1 Preheat the oven to 400°F (200°C). Butter a medium baking dish.

2 Pour water into the bottom of a steaming pot and bring to a boil over high heat. Place the whole cauliflower on a steamer rack over (not touching) the water, cover, and steam until nearly fork-tender, 15–20 minutes. Transfer the cauliflower to a cutting board, let cool until it can be handled, and then cut lengthwise into 8 spearlike wedges and arrange in a single layer in the prepared baking dish.

3 In a saucepan, melt 1 tbsp of the butter over medium heat until it foams. Remove from the heat and whisk in the flour. Return the pan to medium heat and slowly add the milk while whisking constantly. Reduce the heat to low, add 1 tsp salt and ½ tsp black pepper, and cook, whisking occasionally, until the taste of flour is gone and the sauce has thickened and is smooth, about 15 minutes.

4 Meanwhile, in a small frying pan, melt the remaining 1 tsp butter over medium heat. Add the bread crumbs and cook, stirring often, until golden, 3–4 minutes. Remove from the heat.

5 Stir the capers and red pepper flakes into the white sauce and pour evenly over the cauliflower. Sprinkle with the toasted crumbs. Bake until the sauce is bubbling and the edges are golden, about 30 minutes. Serve directly from the dish.

MELLOW CAULIFLOWER IS GIVEN A WELCOME BOOST OF FLAVOR WITH THE ADDITION OF SPICY RED PEPPER FLAKES AND BRINY CAPERS.

SERVES
4

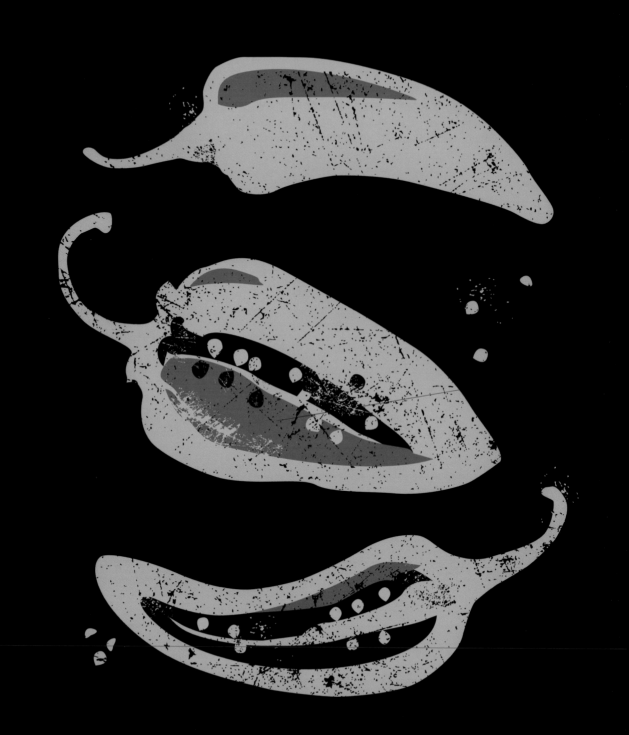

HOT

**SERVES
6**

JALAPEÑO POPPERS

12 small jalapeño chiles

2 thick slices applewood-smoked bacon, chopped

¼ lb (125 g) cream cheese, at room temperature

1 cup (4 oz/125 g) finely shredded Monterey jack cheese

1 tsp hot-pepper sauce

Kosher salt and freshly ground pepper

2 large eggs

1 tbsp whole milk

1 cup (1½ oz/45 g) panko bread crumbs

Canola oil for deep-frying

Ranch dip (optional)

1 Slit each chile on one side from the stem to the tip, then make a partial cut at the base of the stem so there's a "T" cut into the side, leaving the stem end intact. Gently open the chile and remove and discard the seeds.

2 In a frying pan, cook the bacon over medium heat until crisp, about 5 minutes, then drain on paper towels. In a small bowl, mix together the bacon, cream cheese, Monterey jack, and hot sauce, and season with salt and pepper. Using a small spoon, fill the chiles with the cheese mixture, dividing it evenly. Close the filled chiles, pressing the seams firmly to seal.

3 In a shallow bowl, whisk together the eggs and milk. In a second shallow bowl, stir together the crumbs and a pinch each of salt and pepper. One at a time, dip the chiles into the egg mixture, allowing the excess to drip off, and then into the crumbs, patting them gently so they adhere. Transfer to a platter and let dry for 10 minutes, then repeat, dipping the chiles into the egg and then into the crumbs.

4 Pour the oil to a depth of 3 inches (7.5 cm) into a deep, heavy saucepan and heat to 325°F (165°C). Preheat the oven to 200°F (95°C). Line a rimmed baking sheet with paper towels.

5 Working in batches, deep-fry the chiles, turning occasionally, until golden brown, about 6 minutes. Using a wire skimmer, transfer the chiles to the towel-lined pan to drain and then keep warm in the oven while you fry the remaining chiles. Let the poppers cool slightly before serving with ranch dip (if using).

HOT WINGS
WITH BLUE CHEESE DIP

3 lb (1.5 kg) chicken wings, cut at the joint, tips removed

3 tbsp canola oil

2 tbsp Sweet & Smoky BBQ Rub (page 92)

8 garlic cloves

1 cup (8 oz/250 g) sour cream

¼ cup (2 fl oz/60 ml) mayonnaise

1 tbsp *each* Worcestershire sauce and fresh lemon juice

2 tbsp chopped fresh chives

⅛ tsp cayenne pepper

1 cup (5 oz/155 g) crumbled blue cheese

Kosher salt and freshly ground black pepper

½ cup (4 oz/125 g) unsalted butter

½ cup (4 fl oz/125 ml) hot-pepper sauce

1 tbsp distilled white vinegar

1 In a large bowl, combine the wings and oil and toss to coat evenly. Sprinkle the rub over the wings and toss again to coat evenly. Cover and refrigerate overnight.

2 The next day, make the blue cheese dip: Mince 2 of the garlic cloves, then crush to a paste. In a bowl, combine the garlic paste, sour cream, mayonnaise, Worcestershire, lemon juice, chives, and cayenne and mix well. Fold in the cheese, then season with salt and black pepper. Cover and refrigerate until ready to serve.

3 Remove the wings from the refrigerator. Prepare a charcoal or gas grill for high heat. Mince the remaining 6 garlic cloves. In a large frying pan, melt the butter over medium heat, add the garlic, and cook, stirring, until translucent, about 2 minutes. Add the hot sauce and vinegar, stir well, and remove from the heat.

4 Oil the grill grates. Place the wings on the grill rack directly over the fire and cook, turning them frequently, until browned on all sides, slightly charred, and tender, 15–20 minutes. Transfer the wings to the hot sauce in the frying pan, place the pan over low heat, and toss the wings to coat evenly. Let the wings and the sauce sit for 5 minutes.

5 Transfer the wings to a platter and pour any sauce in the pan over the top. Serve with the blue cheese dip.

THIS GRILLED VERSION OF THE FAMED BUFFALO WINGS CARRIES HEAT IN BOTH THE RUB AND THE SAUCE. THE COOLING CLASSIC BLUE CHEESE DIP IS A MUST.

SERVES
6–8

CHILE CON QUESO

7 Anaheim chiles

2–4 jalapeño chiles, plus sliced rounds for garnish

2 tbsp unsalted butter

2 small white onions, finely chopped

2 tomatoes, chopped

1 cup (8 fl oz/250 ml) heavy cream

Kosher salt

1 lb (500 g) queso Oaxaca or Monterey jack cheese, shredded

Tortilla chips

1 Roast, peel, and seed the Anaheim chiles as directed on page 15, then cut into long, narrow strips. Stem the jalapeño chiles, slit lengthwise, remove and discard the seeds, and cut into long, narrow strips.

2 In a large frying pan, melt the butter over medium heat. Add the onions and jalapeño chiles and cook, stirring, until the onions are soft and golden, about 5 minutes. Stir in the Anaheim chiles and tomatoes and cook, stirring, until all of the chiles are soft, about 5 minutes longer. Pour in the cream and 1/4 cup (2 fl oz/60 ml) warm water, season with salt, stir well, and simmer for 3–5 minutes to blend the flavors.

3 Stir in the cheese, cover, and remove from the heat. When the cheese has melted, stir well to combine, pour the contents of the pan into a serving bowl, sprinkle with a few jalapeño slices, and serve with tortilla chips for dipping.

OYSTERS WITH GINGER-CHILE SALSA

2 tbsp minced fresh ginger

1–2 jalapeño or serrano chiles, seeded (optional) and minced

¼ cup (¾ oz/20 g) chopped green onion

1½ cups (9 oz/280 g) chopped tomato

Juice of 1 lime

1 tbsp soy sauce

1 tsp toasted sesame oil

Kosher salt

48 large oysters in the shell, scrubbed

1 In a bowl, stir together the ginger, chiles, green onion, tomato, lime juice, soy sauce, and sesame oil. Season with salt.

2 Discard any oyster whose shell does not close to the touch. Using an oven mitt or work gloves to protect your hand, shuck each oyster, removing the top shell and leaving the oyster and its liquor in the bottom shell. Spoon a little of the salsa onto each oyster. Serve with the remaining salsa alongside.

SERRANO CHILES ARE A LITTLE HOTTER THAN JALAPEÑOS, SO CHOOSE THE LATTER FOR THIS ASIAN-INSPIRED SALSA IF YOU'RE SENSITIVE. ANY EXTRA SALSA IS DELICIOUS SPOONED OVER GRILLED FISH.

SERVES
6–8

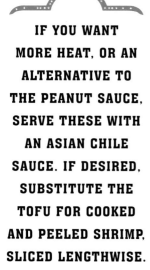

IF YOU WANT
MORE HEAT, OR AN
ALTERNATIVE TO
THE PEANUT SAUCE,
SERVE THESE WITH
AN ASIAN CHILE
SAUCE. IF DESIRED,
SUBSTITUTE THE
TOFU FOR COOKED
AND PEELED SHRIMP,
SLICED LENGTHWISE.

SERVES
4–6

VIETNAMESE SPRING ROLLS

12 butter lettuce leaves

12 rice paper rounds, 8–12 inches (20–30 cm) in diameter

2 tbsp *each* thinly shredded fresh mint leaves and basil leaves

2 avocados, pitted, peeled, and sliced lengthwise

¾ lb (375 g) baked tofu, cut into matchsticks

6 green onions, thinly sliced

1 jalapeño chile, seeded and thinly sliced

Spicy Peanut Sauce (page 93)

1 Remove and discard the ribs from the lettuce leaves, then tear into small pieces. Lay a damp kitchen towel on a work surface. Immerse a rice paper round in a shallow bowl of hot water until it bends, 2–3 seconds, then lay it flat on the towel. Place a few pieces of lettuce in a row along the center of the rice paper, leaving 1–2 inches (2.5–5 cm) uncovered on either side. Arrange a few mint and basil leaves, avocado slices, tofu, green onions, and jalapeños in a line along the lettuce.

2 Bring the edge of the round closest to you up and over the filling, tucking it under the filling, and compact the roll gently but firmly, like a burrito. Place the roll, seam side down, on a large platter. Repeat with the remaining ingredients to make 12 rolls total, reheating the water as you go. Cover the rolls with the damp towel and set aside for up to 2 hours.

3 To serve, using a serrated knife, cut each roll in half and arrange on a large platter with the peanut sauce for dipping.

HARISSA POTATOES

¼ cup (2 fl oz/60 ml) canola oil

2 tbsp harissa, homemade (page 88) or purchased

¼ tsp cayenne pepper

1 tbsp sesame seeds

Kosher salt and freshly ground black pepper

3 lb (1.5 kg) russet potatoes, peeled and cut into 2-inch (5-cm) chunks

1 cup (8 oz/250 g) plain Greek yogurt

Leaves from ½ bunch fresh mint, finely sliced

1 tbsp fresh lemon juice

1 Drizzle the oil evenly into a roasting pan large enough to hold the potatoes in a single layer and place the pan in the oven. Preheat the oven to 425°F (220°C).

2 In a large bowl, stir together the harissa, cayenne, sesame seeds, and 1 tsp salt. Add the potatoes and toss to coat evenly.

3 When the oven is fully preheated, remove the hot roasting pan and carefully add the potatoes, tossing them gently in the oil to coat evenly. Spread the potatoes in a single layer and roast until the undersides are nicely browned, 25–30 minutes. Using a spatula, flip the potatoes and then continue to roast until tender when pierced with a knife and browned and crisp on all sides, about 15 minutes longer.

4 Meanwhile, in a small bowl, stir together the yogurt, most of the mint, and lemon juice. Season with salt and black pepper.

5 Transfer the potatoes to a bowl and serve with the yogurt sauce, sprinkled with the remaining mint leaves, on the side.

THESE POTATOES GET A DOUBLE DOSE OF FIRE FROM CAYENNE PEPPER AND NORTH AFRICAN HARISSA. TO COUNTER THE HEAT, THEY ARE DIPPED INTO A COOLING YOGURT SAUCE.

SERVES 4–6

ANY LARGE, MEXICAN-
INSPIRED MEAL
ISN'T COMPLETE
WITHOUT A SIDE OF
WARM AND SPICY,
LONG-COOKED BEANS.
HOT, BRIGHTLY ACIDIC
SERRANO CHILES
IMPART A BLAZE
OF HEAT TO THIS
VERSION, WHICH ALSO
FEATURES CHOPPED
MEXICAN-STYLE
CACTUS PADS.

SERVES
4

PINTO BEANS
WITH CHILES & NOPALES

1 cup (7 oz/220 g) dried pinto beans

3 tbsp canola oil

1 white onion, finely chopped

1 garlic clove, minced

Kosher salt

3 serrano chiles, stemmed

1 can (14½ oz/455 g) diced
tomatoes, with juice

2 cups (12 oz/375 g) drained canned
nopales (cactus pads), well rinsed
and diced

2 large fresh epazote sprigs
or 1 tsp dried

1 Pick over the beans, discarding any grit or misshapen beans. Rinse well, place in a large saucepan, and add water to cover generously. Bring to a boil, then reduce the heat until the water is barely simmering.

2 Meanwhile, in a small frying pan, warm 1 tbsp of the oil over medium heat. Add half of the onion and cook, stirring until softened, about 4 minutes. Stir in the garlic and cook for 1 minute. Add the onion and garlic to the beans. Cover partially and continue to cook the beans, stirring occasionally and adding hot water as needed to keep the beans covered by 1 inch (2.5 cm), until just tender, about 2 hours.

3 Add 1 tsp salt and continue to cook until the beans are soft, about 40 minutes longer. Reserve ½ cup (4 fl oz/125 ml) of the bean broth. Drain the beans. Set the beans and broth aside.

4 Meanwhile, in a large frying pan, warm the remaining 2 tbsp oil over medium heat. Add the remaining onion and the chiles and sauté until the onion is translucent, about 3 minutes. Remove from the heat, transfer the chiles to a blender, add the tomatoes and juice, and whirl to a slightly chunky purée. Mix the purée into the sautéed onion, return the pan to medium-high heat, and cook, stirring often, until reduced, about 5 minutes. Add the nopales and epazote, season with salt, and bring to a boil. Stir in the beans and reserved broth and simmer until heated through. Transfer to a serving dish and serve.

RED CHILAQUILES
WITH SCRAMBLED EGGS

Canola oil for frying

12 corn tortillas, torn into strips

1 white onion, diced

2 garlic cloves, finely chopped

2 tomatoes, diced

⅓–½ cup (3–4 fl oz/80–125 ml)
Red Chile Sauce (page 91)

¼ cup (⅓ oz/10 g) coarsely chopped
fresh cilantro, plus cilantro leaves

2 tsp unsalted butter

6 large eggs, beaten

1½ cups (10½ oz/330 g)
home-cooked or canned
black beans, heated

Salsa Fresca (page 90)

Sliced jalapeño chiles

Hot-pepper sauce

Crema

Crumbled Cotija cheese (optional)

1 Pour the oil to a depth of 1 inch (2.5 cm) into a large, deep frying pan and heat to 350°F (180°C). Line a large rimmed baking sheet with paper towels. Working in batches, fry the tortilla strips until crisp, 2–3 minutes. Using a slotted spoon, transfer to the towel-lined pan to drain.

2 Pour off all but 2 tbsp of the oil from the pan and return the pan to medium heat. Add the onion and cook, stirring, until it begins to soften, about 1 minute. Add the garlic and tomatoes and cook for 1 minute longer. Return the tortillas to the pan and stir in ⅓ cup (3 fl oz/80 ml) of the chile sauce, adding more sauce if needed to soften and generously coat the strips. Cook, stirring often, until the tortillas are heated through and have absorbed the sauce, about 3 minutes. Stir in the chopped cilantro.

3 Meanwhile, in another frying pan, melt the butter over medium heat. Add the eggs and cook, stirring often, until they have formed soft, moist scrambled curds.

4 Divide the tortilla mixture among plates and top each serving with a large spoonful of hot beans, some scrambled eggs, and a dollop of salsa, and garnish with the jalapeño slices and cilantro leaves. Serve with the hot sauce, crema, and cheese (if using).

THIS TRADITIONAL MEXICAN BREAKFAST DISH OF SCRAMBLED EGGS AND CRISPY TORTILLAS IS ALWAYS POPULAR. IF YOU DON'T FEEL LIKE FRYING, YOU CAN ALSO USE PURCHASED TORTILLA CHIPS.

SERVES
4

NOT ALL CURRY PASTES ARE CREATED EQUAL, SO SEARCH OUT A BRAND THAT YOU LIKE AND ADJUST THE AMOUNT ACCORDINGLY. A WIDE SELECTION, AS WELL AS TAMARIND PASTE, IS AVAILABLE AT MOST ASIAN GROCERY STORES.

SERVES
2–4

COCONUT CURRY SEAFOOD SOUP

2 tbsp canola oil

⅓–½ cup (3–5 oz/90–155 g) Thai red curry paste

2 cans (14 fl oz/430 ml each) coconut milk

¼ cup (2 fl oz/60 ml) fish sauce

2 tbsp fresh lime juice

2 tbsp firmly packed brown sugar

1 tbsp tamarind paste

1 lb (500 g) dried flat rice noodles

1 lb (500 g) clams, scrubbed

½ lb (250 g) cleaned squid, with tubes cut into ½-inch (12-mm) rings

½ lb (250 g) large shrimp, peeled with tails intact and deveined

Mung bean sprouts

Fresh cilantro sprigs

Thai or sweet basil sprigs

Thinly sliced green onion

Thinly sliced serrano chile

Lime wedges

1 In a large pot with a tight-fitting lid, warm the oil over medium-high heat. Add the curry paste and cook, stirring constantly, until fragrant, about 1 minute. Stir in the coconut milk, 1½ cups (12 fl oz/375 ml) water, the fish sauce, lime juice, brown sugar, and tamarind paste. Reduce the heat to medium-low and simmer to blend the flavors.

2 Meanwhile, bring a pot of water to a boil over high heat. Add the noodles and cook, stirring to separate, until tender, 4–5 minutes. Drain the noodles and rinse with cold water. Divide the noodles among the serving bowls.

3 Add the clams to the pot of coconut mixture, cover, and cook until they just start to open, about 1 minute. Add the squid and shrimp, stirring slightly to coat with the coconut mixture, and cover the pot again. Cook until the clams are completely opened and the squid and shrimp are opaque, about 3 minutes longer. Discard any clams that did not open. Spoon the seafood and broth over the noodles and serve with mung beans, cilantro, basil, green onion, chile, and lime wedges on the side.

TEXAS BABY BACK RIBS

¾ cup (6 fl oz/180 ml) *each* white wine vinegar and apple cider vinegar

⅓ cup (3 fl oz/80 ml) Worcestershire sauce

2 tbsp ground New Mexico chile

1 tbsp dried Mexican oregano

2 tsp hot paprika

1 tsp *each* garlic salt, garlic powder, onion salt, and onion powder

1 tsp *each* coriander and cumin seeds, toasted and ground

1 tsp dry mustard

½ tsp ground allspice

½ tsp ground cinnamon

1 tbsp puréed chipotle chiles in adobo sauce

½ cup (4 fl oz/125 ml) chili sauce

½ cup (3½ oz/105 g) firmly packed dark brown sugar

¼ cup (2 fl oz/60 ml) tamarind paste

¼ cup (3 oz/90 g) honey

3 slabs baby back ribs, about 5 lb (2.5 kg) total, trimmed

1 In a bowl, combine the vinegars, Worcestershire, New Mexico chile, oregano, paprika, garlic salt and powder, onion salt and powder, coriander, cumin, mustard, allspice, cinnamon, chipotle purée, chili sauce, brown sugar, tamarind paste, and honey. Mix well, then pour half of the sauce into a large baking dish. Add the ribs and turn the slabs to coat well. Pour over the remaining sauce, cover, and refrigerate overnight.

2 Preheat the oven to 350°F (180°C). Line a large rimmed baking sheet with aluminum foil. Place a large wire rack on the lined pan. Remove the ribs from the sauce, reserving the sauce. Place the ribs, meaty side up, on the rack. Bake, basting with ¼ cup (2 fl oz/60 ml) sauce once every 30 minutes, until the ribs are tender, about 1¼ hours.

3 Pour the remaining sauce into a saucepan, bring to a boil over high heat, reduce the heat to medium, and simmer until thickened, 25–30 minutes. Keep warm.

4 Let the rib slabs rest for 10 minutes, then cut them into individual ribs, pile the ribs on a platter, and serve with the heated sauce on the side.

TEXAS COOKS LIKE THE SAUCE ON THEIR PORK RIBS TO BE BOTH COMPLEX AND SPICY HOT. AND THEY LIKE TO MODERATE THE FIRE WITH A BIG BATCH OF COLESLAW.

SERVES
6

A CLASSIC OF NORTH AFRICA, THIS SPICY TOMATO AND EGG DISH IS GREAT FOR LUNCH OR DINNER. FOR A MEDIUM-HOT VERSION, TRY HALF HOT AND HALF SWEET PAPRIKA.

SERVES
4

SHAKSHOUKA

1 tbsp hot or sweet paprika

1¼ tsp ground coriander

1 tsp ground cumin

3 tbsp extra-virgin olive oil

1 cup (4 oz/125 g) coarsely chopped white onion

2 large garlic cloves, minced

1 jalapeño chile, sliced

1¼ lb (625 g) firm but ripe tomatoes, coarsely chopped

3 tbsp tomato paste

Kosher salt and freshly ground pepper

4 large eggs

¼ cup (⅓ oz/10 g) coarsely chopped fresh flat-leaf parsley

Warmed pita bread

1 In a large, dry frying pan with a lid, toast the paprika, coriander, and cumin over medium heat, stirring often, until fragrant, about 1 minute. Add 2 tbsp of the oil and swirl the pan to combine the oil with the spices and heat evenly. Add the onion and cook, stirring often, until softened and starting to brown, 8–10 minutes. Add the garlic and chile and cook, stirring, until fragrant, about 1 minute. Add the tomatoes, tomato paste, 1¼ tsp salt, and ⅓ cup (3 fl oz/80 ml) water and stir well. Reduce the heat to low and simmer for 15–20 minutes to blend the flavors. Taste and adjust the seasoning.

2 Using the back of a spoon, make 4 wells in the tomato mixture, spacing them evenly apart. Crack 1 egg into each well and lightly season the eggs with salt and pepper. Cover and cook until the egg whites are set and the yolks are still a little runny, about 5 minutes.

3 Uncover and drizzle with the remaining 1 tbsp oil and sprinkle with the parsley. Serve right away directly from the pan, accompanied with pita bread.

PUNGENT AND EYE-
WATERING WASABI,
A POTENT COUSIN
OF HOT MUSTARD,
ADDS BRIGHT, HOT
FLAVOR TO BOTH THE
DIPPING SAUCE AND
THE COATING FOR
THESE DELECTABLE
SCALLOPS.

SERVES
6

WASABI SCALLOPS

½ cup (4 fl oz/125 ml) sake, mirin,
or sweet sherry

3 tbsp wasabi paste or powder

1 tbsp minced fresh ginger

3–4 tbsp soy sauce, plus more as needed

24 large sea scallops

Toasted sesame oil for brushing

Peanut oil or canola oil for coating

1 In a small bowl, stir together the sake, 1 tbsp of the wasabi paste, the ginger, and 1 tbsp of the soy sauce. Set the sauce aside.

2 Lay the scallops on a platter and brush them generously on all sides with sesame oil. In a small bowl, stir together the remaining 2 tbsp wasabi paste and 2 tbsp of the soy sauce, adding more soy sauce if needed to thin to a brushing consistency. Brush the scallops generously on all sides with the mixture. Let the scallops sit for 15–30 minutes before grilling. Prepare a charcoal or gas grill for high heat.

3 Oil the grill grates (or, if you fear the scallops may fall through the bars of the grill rack, oil a grilling basket or grid.) Place the scallops on the grill rack directly over the fire and cook, turning once, until firm and opaque, 3–4 minutes total. Transfer the scallops to a platter and serve with the wasabi-sake sauce for dipping.

PORK VINDALOO

2 1/2–3 lb (1.25–1.5 kg) boneless pork shoulder

Kosher salt and freshly ground black pepper

1/2 cup (4 fl oz/125 ml) canola oil

2 yellow onions, finely chopped

8 garlic cloves, minced

2-inch (5-cm) piece fresh ginger, grated

2 tsp cayenne pepper

1 1/2 tsp *each* brown mustard seeds, ground cumin, hot paprika, and ground turmeric

1/2 tsp ground cinnamon

Pinch of ground cloves

1/3 cup (3 fl oz/80 ml) white wine vinegar

1 cup (8 fl oz/250 ml) chicken broth

1 Trim the pork of excess fat, then cut into 1-inch (2.5-cm) cubes. Place in a bowl, sprinkle with 1 tsp each salt and black pepper, and toss to coat. In a large Dutch oven or heavy pot, warm the oil over medium-high heat. Working in batches, add the pork and cook until well browned on all sides, 6–7 minutes. Transfer the pork to a large plate.

2 Add the onions to the fat remaining in the pot, raise the heat to high, and cook, stirring, until browned, 10–12 minutes. Add the garlic, ginger, cayenne, mustard seeds, cumin, paprika, turmeric, cinnamon, and cloves and cook, stirring, until the spices are fragrant and evenly coat the onions, about 1 minute. Pour in the vinegar and deglaze the pan, scraping up the browned bits on the pan bottom with a wooden spoon. Stir in the broth and bring to a boil.

3 Return the pork to the pot, cover, reduce the heat to low, and cook until the pork is very tender, 1 1/2–2 hours.

4 Transfer to a serving bowl and serve.

VINDALOOS, A SPECIALTY OF CENTRAL AND SOUTHWESTERN COASTAL INDIA, ARE THE MOST MOUTH SEARING OF THE CURRY DISHES. THIS ONE IS TAME BY ANY MEASURE, SO FEEL FREE TO UP THE CAYENNE IF AUTHENTICITY IS YOUR GOAL.

SERVES
6

MAC 'N' CHEESE
WITH JALAPEÑO CREAM

2 tbsp unsalted butter, plus butter for the baking dish

Kosher salt

¾ lb (375 g) dried elbow macaroni

2 cups (16 fl oz/500 ml) milk

1–2 jalapeño chiles, seeded and chopped

1½ tbsp all-purpose flour

½ lb (250 g) pepper jack or Monterey jack cheese, shredded

¼ tsp red pepper flakes (optional)

1 Preheat the oven to 375°F (190°C). Butter a 2-qt (2-l) baking dish. Bring a large pot three-fourths full of salted water to a boil over high heat. Add the macaroni, stir well, and cook until al dente, according to the package directions. Drain the pasta and set aside.

2 Meanwhile, in a saucepan, combine the milk and chiles and warm over medium heat until small bubbles appear along the sides of the pan. Remove from the heat and let sit for 5–25 minutes, depending on the desired heat level, tasting often. Strain the milk, reserving the chiles and the milk.

3 In a large saucepan, melt the butter over medium heat. Whisk in the flour and 1½ tsp salt and cook, whisking constantly, until the flour smells toasted, about 1 minute. Slowly add the milk, ¼ cup (2 fl oz/60 ml) at a time, while whisking constantly to break up any lumps. When all of the milk is incorporated, continue to whisk until the mixture thickens slightly, about 3 minutes.

4 Add the reserved pasta and half of the cheese and stir to mix well. Transfer to the prepared baking dish and sprinkle with the remaining cheese, the reserved chiles, and the red pepper flakes (if using). Bake until bubbling and browned on top, about 30 minutes. Let sit for a few minutes before serving.

WHAT'S BETTER THAN TRADITIONAL MACARONI AND CHEESE? HOW ABOUT MACARONI AND CHEESE WITH A KICK. IT'S FANTASTIC ALONGSIDE FRIED CHICKEN.

SERVES
6

THESE PORK KEBABS
HAVE A CARIBBEAN
VIBE THANKS TO
THE CHIPOTLE-LIME
MARINADE. SERVE
THEM WITH A SIDE
OF BLACK BEANS
AND RICE.

SERVES
4–6

PORK KEBABS
WITH CHIPOTLE MARINADE

1 can (14 fl oz/430 ml) coconut milk

1 bunch fresh cilantro

2 garlic cloves, crushed

1 chipotle chile in adobo sauce

1 tbsp ground coriander

1 tsp red pepper flakes

Kosher salt and freshly ground
black pepper

Lime wedges

2 pork tenderloins, 1½ lb (750 g)
each, cut into 1-inch (2.5-cm) cubes

2 sweet potatoes, peeled and cut
into 1-inch (2.5-cm) cubes

1 In a blender or food processor, whirl the coconut milk, cilantro, garlic, chipotle chile, coriander, and red pepper flakes until smooth. Add 1 tsp black pepper and a squeeze of lime juice and pulse to blend. Season with salt and with more lime juice if needed. Put the pork cubes and marinade in a large sealable container, pour in the marinade, and seal the container closed. Refrigerate for at least 4 hours or preferably overnight.

2 About 30 minutes before you are ready to grill, remove the pork from the refrigerator and discard the marinade, but do not pat the meat dry. Soak 6–12 wooden skewers in water. Prepare a charcoal or gas grill for high heat.

3 In a saucepan, combine the sweet potatoes with water to cover, bring to a boil over high heat, and cook for 5 minutes. Drain and let cool. Then, alternating the pork and potato cubes, thread them onto the skewers, leaving a little space between the cubes.

4 Oil the grill grates. Place the skewers on the grill rack directly over the fire and cook, turning the skewers after about 5 minutes, until the pork and potatoes have grill marks, the pork feels just firm to the touch, and the sweet potatoes are tender, about 10 minutes total.

5 Transfer the skewers to a platter, let rest for 5 minutes, and serve with lime wedges.

SHORT RIBS
WITH ANCHO CHILE SAUCE

2 ancho chiles, stemmed, seeded, and torn into pieces

4 lb (2 kg) English-cut beef short ribs

Kosher salt and freshly ground black pepper

¼ cup (2 fl oz/60 ml) canola oil

1 tsp red pepper flakes

1 yellow onion, chopped

1 green bell pepper, seeded and chopped

2 garlic cloves, minced

2 chipotle chiles in adobo sauce, chopped

2 tbsp fresh lemon juice

1 tomato, seeded and chopped

Hot cooked soft polenta

1 Put the chiles in a heatproof bowl, add boiling water to cover, and let soak until soft, about 15 minutes. Drain and set aside.

2 Season the ribs all over with salt and black pepper. In a large frying pan, warm the oil over medium-high heat. Working in batches to avoid crowding, add the ribs and cook, turning frequently, until browned on all sides, about 10 minutes. Transfer to a plate. Preheat the oven to 325°F (165°C).

3 Pour off all but 1 tbsp of the fat from the pan and return the pan to medium-high heat. Add the reserved ancho chiles, pepper flakes, onion, bell pepper, garlic, chipotle chiles, lemon juice, tomato, 1 tsp salt, and ½ tsp black pepper and cook, stirring, until the onion and bell pepper have softened, 8–10 minutes. Transfer to a food processor or blender, add 1 cup (8 fl oz/250 ml) water, and whirl until the mixture is thick and nearly smooth.

4 Arrange the ribs in a single layer in a roasting pan. Add the chile mixture, turn the ribs to coat well, cover, and place in the oven. Cook, turning the ribs several times, until very tender, about 3 hours, stirring in more water as needed to keep the sauce moist.

5 Spoon polenta onto individual plates, top with ribs, spoon some sauce over them, and serve.

SWEET, MILD ANCHOS ARE MIXED WITH SMOKY CHIPOTLES IN THIS INTENSELY FLAVORED SAUCE FOR FALL-OFF-THE-BONE-TENDER RIBS. SERVE WITH POLENTA TO INCREASE THE INDULGENCE FACTOR.

SERVES
4–6

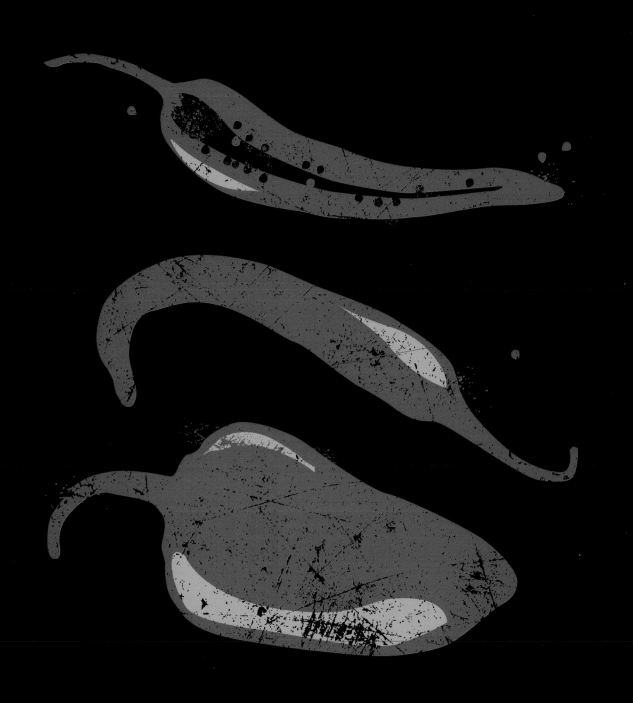

FIERY

SPICY CRAB SALAD

1¼ lb (625 g) lump crabmeat

1 Thai chile, finely chopped

Grated zest of 2 limes

Juice of 1 lime, plus 2 tbsp

2 tbsp coarsely chopped fresh mint

2 tbsp mayonnaise

Kosher salt and freshly
ground pepper

6 tbsp (3 fl oz/90 ml) extra-virgin
olive oil

2 heads red or white Belgian endive

2 bunches watercress

2 green onions, thinly sliced
on the diagonal

3 avocados, pitted, peeled,
and sliced lengthwise

1 Pat the crabmeat dry and place in a bowl. Add the chile, lime zest, juice of 1 lime, mint, and mayonnaise. Stir gently to combine. Season with salt, cover, and refrigerate while you prepare the rest of the salad.

2 In a small bowl, whisk together the oil and the remaining 2 tbsp lime juice. Season with salt and pepper and set the dressing aside.

3 Trim the endives, separate the leaves, and cut them into 1-inch (2.5-cm) strips. Trim the tough stems from the watercress. Put the endives and watercress in a bowl, add the green onions, drizzle with the dressing, and toss to coat evenly.

4 Divide the greens among individual salad plates and arrange a few avocado slices on each portion. Spoon some of the crabmeat mixture onto each plate, garnish with a few cracks of pepper, and serve.

THAI CHILES, ALSO
KNOWN AS BIRD'S
EYE CHILES, ARE
TINY BUT SUPERHOT
SO PROCEED WITH
CAUTION. IF CRAB
ISN'T IN SEASON,
YOU CAN SUBSTITUTE
COOKED SHRIMP WITH
DELICIOUS RESULTS.

SERVES
4–6

SICHUAN DISHES ARE
KNOWN FOR BEING
FIERY HOT AND
DEEPLY FLAVORFUL,
AND THIS CLASSIC
DOESN'T DISAPPOINT.
LOOK FOR JARRED
BLACK BEAN PASTE
LIBERALLY SPECKLED
WITH CHILE FLAKES.

SERVES
4

MAPO TOFU

1 package (14 oz/440 g) soft tofu

¾ cup (6 fl oz/180 ml) chicken broth

2 tbsp hot black bean paste

1 tbsp soy sauce

2 tbsp canola oil

½ lb (250 g) ground lean pork

1 tbsp minced garlic

2 tbsp minced fresh ginger

½ red Fresno or serrano chile, sliced

2 tbsp cornstarch

1 tsp ground Sichuan pepper

2 green onions, thinly sliced
on the diagonal

Hot cooked rice

1 Drain the tofu, cut into bite-size cubes, put in a heatproof bowl, and add boiling water to cover. In a small bowl, stir together the broth, bean paste, and soy sauce. Set the 2 bowls aside.

2 Heat a wok or large frying pan over high heat, pour in the oil, and swirl to coat the pan. Add the pork and cook, breaking up any lumps, until it starts to brown, about 6 minutes. Add the garlic and ginger and cook, stirring, until fragrant, about 2 minutes. Add the chile and stir to mix.

3 Stir the bean sauce mixture to recombine, then add it to the pork and bring to a simmer. Meanwhile, in a small bowl, stir together the cornstarch and 2 tbsp water. Add the cornstarch mixture to the pan and bring to a boil, stirring gently. Cook, stirring, until thickened and glossy, about 30 seconds. Drain the tofu, then slide it into the sauce and stir gently just to coat, being careful not to break up the cubes.

4 Transfer to a serving dish. Sprinkle with the Sichuan pepper and green onions and serve, accompanied with the rice.

THERE ARE A FEW
VARIETIES OF ASIAN-
STYLE EGGPLANT.
LOOK FOR LONG AND
THIN VEGETABLES
WITH ANY SHADE
OF PURPLE, AND
AVOID THE LARGE,
ROUND, FLESH-DENSE
AUBERGINE VARIETY
FOR THIS DISH.

SERVES
4

GRILLED EGGPLANT
WITH SPICY CHILE SAUCE

1 tbsp canola oil, plus more
for brushing

1 shallot, minced

2 garlic cloves, minced

1 hot red chile, preferably
Thai, minced

1/3 cup (3 fl oz/80 ml) fish sauce

Juice of 1 lime

1 tbsp firmly packed brown sugar

6 Asian eggplants,
halved lengthwise

Hot cooked rice

3 tbsp slivered fresh Thai
or sweet basil leaves

1 Prepare a charcoal or gas grill for indirect high heat by either building the coals to one side of the charcoal grill or turning half the burners off on a gas grill.

2 In a large frying pan, warm the 1 tbsp oil over medium-high heat. Add the shallot, garlic, and chile and cook, stirring, until the shallot softens but does not brown, about 1 minute. Remove from the heat, add the fish sauce, lime juice, and brown sugar, and stir to dissolve the sugar. Set aside.

3 Brush the eggplants on both sides with oil. Oil the grill grates. Place the eggplants on the grill rack over the unheated area of the fire. Cook, covered, turning occasionally, until tender, about 6 minutes.

4 Remove the eggplants from the grill, chop into 1-inch (2.5-cm) chunks, and add to the sauce. Stir gently to combine. Spoon the rice into individual bowls, top with the eggplant and sauce, sprinkle with the basil, and serve.

HOT & SOUR SOUP
WITH SHRIMP & THAI CHILES

¾ lb (375 g) large shrimp

3 lemongrass stalks

5 thin slices galangal, about ¼ inch (6 mm) thick

3 fresh or dried lime leaves, or grated zest of 1 lime

2 tbsp fish sauce

5 oz (155 g) white mushrooms, trimmed and caps quartered

1 tomato, peeled and cut into thin wedges

¼ small yellow onion, thinly sliced lengthwise

4 tsp Thai red or green chile paste

2 small chiles such as Thai or serrano

¼ cup (2 fl oz/60 ml) fresh lime juice

¼ cup (⅓ oz/10 g) chopped fresh cilantro

1 Peel the shrimp, with the tail segments intact, and reserve the shells. Devein the shrimp and refrigerate until ready to use. In a large saucepan, combine the shrimp shells with 5 cups (40 fl oz/1.25 l) water. Trim off and discard the root end and grassy tops from each lemongrass stalk, then smash the bulb portion, cut into 1-inch (2.5-cm) lengths, and add to the pan. Bring to a simmer over medium heat, cover partially, and simmer gently for 15 minutes to blend the flavors. Strain the broth through a fine-mesh sieve into a clean saucepan.

2 Add the galangal, lime leaves, fish sauce, mushrooms, tomato, onion, and chile paste to the broth. Stem the chiles, quarter them lengthwise, and add as many of the quarters to the broth as you like; you may want to start with just a few.

3 Bring the soup to a simmer over medium heat, cover partially, and simmer gently until the mushrooms are barely tender, about 2 minutes. Taste halfway through and add more chile quarters if the soup is not spicy enough. Stir in the shrimp and simmer just until they turn pink, about 2 minutes. Remove from the heat. Stir in the lime juice and cilantro.

4 Ladle into bowls and serve.

THIS SOUTHEAST ASIAN FAVORITE, CALLED TOM YUM GOONG, RELIES ON BOTH FRESH CHILES AND CHILE PASTE FOR ITS SIGNATURE FIRE.

SERVES
6

JERK CHICKEN

3 green onions, chopped

4 large garlic cloves, chopped

3 Scotch bonnet chiles, chopped

¼ cup (2 fl oz/60 ml) fresh lime juice

3 tbsp extra-virgin olive oil

2 tbsp tamari or soy sauce

1 tbsp firmly packed brown sugar

1 tbsp chopped fresh thyme

2 tsp ground allspice

1 tsp ground nutmeg

½ tsp ground cinnamon

Kosher salt and freshly ground pepper

6 whole chicken legs, cut at the joint

Chopped fresh cilantro

Lime halves

1 In a blender or food processor, whirl the green onions, garlic, chiles, lime juice, oil, tamari, brown sugar, thyme, allspice, nutmeg, cinnamon, and 2 teaspoons each salt and pepper until smooth. Taste and adjust the seasoning with salt and pepper. Put the chicken in a shallow dish and coat evenly on all sides with the mixture (wear rubber gloves if using your hands). Cover and refrigerate for at least 8 hours or up to overnight.

2 Prepare a charcoal or gas grill for indirect medium heat by either building the coals to one side of the charcoal grill or turning half the burners off on a gas grill.

3 Oil the grill grates. Place the chicken on the grill rack directly over the heat. Cook, covered, turning once, until nicely browned on both sides, about 2 minutes on each side. Move the chicken to the indirect-heat area and cook, covered, until cooked through, about 30 minutes.

4 Transfer the chicken to a platter, tent with foil, and let stand for 10 minutes. Sprinkle the chicken with cilantro and serve with lime halves.

AUTHENTIC JERK DISHES INCLUDE BOTH SCOTCH BONNET CHILES AND ALLSPICE. BUT BEYOND THAT, EVERY JAMAICAN COOK'S RECIPE IS A BIT DIFFERENT. THIS DISH IS MEANT TO BE SEARINGLY HOT, BUT IF YOU WANT TO TAME THE SPICE A BIT, REMOVE THE SEEDS FROM THE CHILES.

SERVES
4–6

THIS HOMEY NOODLE DISH, KNOWN AS DANDAN MIAN, PACKS A PUNCH, THANKS TO THE USE OF CHILE OIL AND FRESH CHILES. THE CREAMY TEXTURE COMES FROM THE FLOUR IN THE FRESH NOODLES AND THE SESAME PASTE.

SERVES
6

SESAME NOODLES
WITH PEANUTS & THAI CHILES

½ cup (4 fl oz/120 ml) canola oil

⅓ cup (2 oz/60 g) raw peanuts

Kosher salt

7 oz (220 g) fresh Chinese flat wheat noodles

¼ cup (2½ oz/75 g) Chinese sesame paste

2 tbsp chile oil

2 tbsp toasted sesame oil

2 tbsp soy sauce

½ cup (1½ oz/45 g) chopped green onions

1 Thai chile, chopped

1 Heat a wok or large frying pan over high heat. Pour in ¼ cup (2 fl oz/60 ml) of the canola oil and heat until nearly smoking. Add the peanuts and fry, stirring continually, until golden, about 1 minute. Using a slotted spoon, transfer the peanuts to a cutting board and let cool. Set aside.

2 Bring a saucepan three-fourths full of lightly salted water to a boil over high heat. Add the noodles and cook until barely tender, 3½–4 minutes. Drain in a colander, then rinse under hot running water. Leave in the sink to drain while you make the sauce.

3 In a bowl, combine the sesame paste, chile oil, sesame oil, soy sauce, 1 tsp salt, the remaining ¼ cup canola oil, and ½ cup (4 fl oz/125 ml) hot water. Stir until well mixed, then taste and adjust the seasoning with salt if needed. Transfer the noodles to a bowl, add the sauce, and stir and toss to mix well.

4 Divide the noodles evenly among individual bowls. Top each serving with the fried peanuts, green onions, and chopped chile and serve.

THIS CRISPY, GLAZED CHICKEN DISH ORIGINATED IN HUNAN, A PROVINCE IN SOUTH-CENTRAL CHINA KNOWN FOR ITS INCENDIARY COOKING. YOU CAN FIND MOST OF THESE INGREDIENTS AT AN ASIAN MARKET, INCLUDING THE SICHUAN PEPPER, WHICH IS NOT HOT BUT RATHER SMOKY IN FLAVOR.

SERVES
4

CRISPY CHICKEN
WITH HUNAN-STYLE SPICES

14 oz (440 g) skin-on, boneless chicken thighs, cut into ¾-inch (2-cm) cubes

1 tbsp dark soy sauce

1 tbsp cornstarch

½ cup (4 fl oz/125 ml) chicken broth

1½ tbsp light soy sauce

1 tbsp black vinegar

4 tsp chile oil

1 tbsp sugar

Peanut oil for deep-frying

¾ cup (2½ oz/75 g) chopped green onion

2 Thai chiles, seeded and sliced

1 tbsp grated fresh ginger

1 tbsp crushed garlic

Kosher salt and ground Sichuan pepper

1 In a nonreactive bowl, combine the chicken, dark soy sauce, and cornstarch and mix well. Let sit for 15–30 minutes.

2 In a small bowl, stir together the broth, light soy sauce, vinegar, chile oil, and sugar. Set aside.

3 Pour the oil to a depth of 1 inch (2.5 cm) into a wok or large frying pan and heat to 360°F (185°C). Line a baking sheet with paper towels and set a wire rack on it. Carefully add the chicken to the hot oil, stir to separate the pieces, and fry until golden brown, about 1½ minutes. Using a slotted spoon, transfer to the rack.

4 Pour off all but 2 tbsp of the oil and return the pan to high heat. Add the green onion, chiles, ginger, and garlic and stir-fry until partially wilted, about 30 seconds. Return the chicken to the pan and stir-fry until the ingredients are evenly mixed, about 30 seconds. Pour in the reserved sauce and stir until combined. Reduce the heat to medium-low, cover, and simmer gently until the chicken is tender and the flavors are well blended, about 4 minutes.

5 Season with salt and Sichuan pepper, transfer to a serving dish, and serve.

MEXICAN-STYLE PASTA
WITH THREE CHILES

2 ancho chiles

4 guajillo chiles

4 pasilla chiles

½ tsp cumin seeds

3 garlic cloves, unpeeled

1 tomato

¼ white onion

Kosher salt and freshly ground
pepper

2 tbsp safflower oil

14 oz (440 g) dried fideos
(coiled pasta) or angel hair pasta

2 cups (16 fl oz/500 ml)
chicken broth

¼ cup (2 oz/60 g) sour cream

¼ cup (1½ oz/45 g) crumbled
queso fresco

1 Stem and seed the chiles. Heat a large heavy frying pan over medium heat. Toast the chiles, pressing down firmly for a few seconds with a spatula, and turning often, until softened and fragrant, and then transfer to a bowl. Add very hot water to cover and let soak until soft and pliable, about 15 minutes. Drain and tear into pieces.

2 Meanwhile, toast the cumin seeds in the same pan over medium heat until fragrant, then pour onto a plate. Finally, toast the garlic, tomato, and onion in the same pan over medium heat until the skin of the tomato is blistered and begins to blacken, and the garlic and onion are blackened in spots and begin to soften, about 5 minutes. Let the garlic cool, then peel and discard the skins. In a blender, combine the softened chiles, tomato, onion, garlic, and cumin seeds and whirl until smooth, adding 1 tbsp or so of water if needed to move the blades. Pass through a fine-mesh sieve and season the sauce with salt and pepper.

3 In a large frying pan, warm the oil over medium-high heat. Add the fideos, breaking each coil into thirds. Stir and toss constantly until covered with oil and just beginning to turn golden brown. Add the sauce and cook, stirring often, for 5 minutes, reducing the heat when the sauce begins to bubble. Add the broth and stir until the sauce is absorbed into the pasta and the pasta is tender, about 5 minutes longer. Serve with the sour cream and cheese.

FIDEOS, VERY THIN
MEXICAN-STYLE
PASTA COMMONLY
SERVED AS A SOUP,
ABSORBS THE
HEAT FROM THREE
DIFFERENT DRIED
CHILES—MILD
ANCHOS, MEDIUM
GUAJILLOS, AND FIERY
PASILLAS IN THIS
HOMESTYLE RECIPE.

SERVES
4

KIMCHI FRIED RICE

3 slices bacon, cut into ½-inch (12-mm) pieces, or 3 tbsp oil

2 large eggs, lightly beaten

Kosher salt

2 green onions, sliced on the diagonal

½–1 red Fresno or jalapeño chile, halved lengthwise and sliced crosswise

¼ cup (1¼ oz/40 g) frozen English peas

1 cup (5 oz/155 g) chopped kimchi

1 cup (5 oz/155 g) chilled day-old cooked rice

1 tbsp soy sauce

Sriracha sauce or chile oil

1 Heat a wok or large frying pan over medium-high heat. Add the bacon and cook, stirring occasionally, until crisp, about 5 minutes. Using a slotted spoon, transfer to paper towels to drain. Pour off all but 1 tbsp of the fat (or add 1 tbsp oil if not using bacon) and reserve the remaining fat.

2 Return the pan to medium-high heat and swirl the pan to coat it evenly with the fat. Add the eggs, sprinkle with ¼ tsp salt, and again swirl the pan to spread the eggs evenly into an omelet. Cook, without stirring, until nearly firm but not brown on the edges, about 4 minutes. Using a heat-resistant spatula, fold the omelet into thirds or roll up and transfer to a plate; set aside.

3 Raise the heat to high, add another 1 tbsp fat to the pan, and swirl to coat. Add half of the green onions, the chile, peas, and kimchi and cook, stirring occasionally, until heated through. Add the rice and continue to cook, stirring often, until the mixture starts to brown, about 5 minutes. If the rice starts to stick, make a well in the center of the pan, add a little more fat, and when hot, continue to stir and cook the mixture. Thinly slice the omelet and add to the pan along with the reserved bacon and the soy sauce. Stir and toss to combine.

4 Sprinkle with the remaining green onions and serve right away. Pass Sriracha sauce at the table.

DOZENS OF BRANDS OF KIMCHI (KOREAN-STYLE FERMENTED CABBAGE) ARE AVAILABLE, SO BE SURE TO SEARCH OUT ONE WITH A SPICE LEVEL THAT YOU LIKE FOR THIS EASY-TO-ASSEMBLE DISH.

SERVES
2

HARISSA, A SIZZLING-HOT MOROCCAN CONDIMENT, IS USED HERE IN THREE WAYS: AS A MARINADE, A COATING, AND A TABLE CONDIMENT. THIS RECIPE MAKES MORE HARISSA THAN YOU NEED, BUT THE EXTRA LASTS FOR WEEKS AND IS SO GOOD, IT WON'T BE WASTED.

SERVES
4–6

RACK OF LAMB
WITH HARISSA CRUST

10–12 large guajillo chiles

2 garlic cloves, chopped

½ cup (1½ oz/45 g) dry-packed sun-dried tomatoes, soaked in warm water for 1 hour and drained

½–1 red Fresno or other hot red chile

Kosher salt

1 tsp red wine vinegar

2 tbsp canned tomato paste

1 tbsp ras el hanout (Moroccan spice blend)

¼ cup (2 fl oz/60 ml) extra-virgin olive oil

2 whole lamb racks, 7 to 8 ribs each

1 To make the harissa, stem the guajillo chiles, then grind them in a food processor until the pods will not cut into smaller pieces, about 3 minutes. You need about 1 cup (3½ oz/105 g) total. Toast the chiles in a large, dry frying pan over medium heat, stirring and shaking the pan almost constantly, until fragrant, about 4 minutes.

2 Return the chiles to the processor, add the garlic, tomatoes, Fresno chile, 2 tsp salt, vinegar, tomato paste, ras el hanout, and oil, and process until a smooth, very thick paste forms, about 8 minutes, scraping down the sides of the bowl as needed. Cover and refrigerate for at least 3 hours before using or for up to 3 weeks.

3 Trim the excess fat from the lamb racks and french the bones (or ask the butcher to do it). Slather each rack with about 3 tbsp harissa. Cover and refrigerate for at least 4 hours or for up to 1 day.

4 Remove the lamb from the refrigerator 1 hour before roasting. Preheat the oven to 450°F (230°C). Set the racks, curved bone side down, in a large roasting pan. Spread the meat on each rack with about ⅓ cup (3 fl oz/80 ml) of the harissa.

5 Roast the lamb until the harissa is evenly browned, the bones look crisp, and an instant-read thermometer inserted into the meat registers 140°F (60°C) for medium-rare, about 15 minutes. Transfer to a cutting board, tent with aluminum foil, and let rest for 15 minutes. Cut into individual chops and serve, with more harissa on the side.

Basic Recipes

A pantry well stocked with hot and spicy salsas, condiments, dips, and spreads makes it easy to add heat and spice to anything you cook. Here you'll find a number of all-purpose salsas, a homemade Dijon-style mustard for lending a bite to sandwiches and dressings, lively pickled jalapeños, a zesty horseradish sauce, and more.

SALSA FRESCA

MAKES ABOUT 2 CUPS (16 FL OZ/500 ML)

1 lb (500 g) tomatoes, cut into ¼-inch (6-mm) pieces
⅓ cup (2 oz/60 g) finely chopped white onion
¼ cup (⅓ oz/10 g) chopped fresh cilantro
2 serrano chiles, finely chopped
2 tsp fresh lime juice
Kosher salt

In a bowl, toss together the tomatoes, onion, cilantro, chiles, and lime juice. Season with salt and toss again. If the salsa is too dry, add a splash of water.

Cover and let sit for 10–15 minutes to blend the flavors before serving. Store in an airtight container in the refrigerator for up to 5 days.

SALSA VERDE

MAKES ABOUT 2 CUPS (16 FL OZ/500 ML)

1 lb (500 g) tomatillos, husked and rinsed
3 tbsp coarsely chopped white onion
3 serrano chiles, coarsely chopped
2 garlic cloves, coarsely chopped
Kosher salt
¼ cup (⅓ oz/10 g) chopped fresh cilantro

In a saucepan, combine the tomatillos with water to cover and bring to a gentle boil over medium heat. Cook, uncovered, until soft but not soggy, 8–10 minutes; drain.

In a blender, whirl the tomatillos, onion, chiles, garlic, and ½ tsp salt until a chunky purée forms. Stir in the cilantro and serve. Store in an airtight container in the refrigerator for up to 5 days.

ROASTED CHILE SAUCE

MAKES ABOUT 1 CUP (8 FL OZ/250 ML)

1 red Thai chile
1 red bell pepper
¾ cup (6 fl oz/180 ml) rice vinegar
½ cup (4 oz/125 g) sugar

Roast, peel, and seed the chile and bell pepper as directed on page 15.

In a nonreactive saucepan, combine the vinegar and sugar and bring to a boil over medium-high heat, stirring constantly to dissolve the sugar. Boil the syrup for 5 minutes, then remove from the heat and let cool.

In a blender, whirl the syrup, chile, and bell pepper until smooth. Store in an airtight container in the refrigerator for up to 5 days.

DRUNKEN PASILLA CHILE SALSA

MAKES ABOUT 1½ CUPS (12 FL OZ/375 ML)

5 pasilla chiles
3 garlic cloves, coarsely chopped
1 thin slice white onion, coarsely chopped
1 cup (8 fl oz/250 ml) fresh orange juice
¼ cup (2 fl oz/60 ml) beer or tequila blanco
Kosher salt

Toast the chiles in a heavy frying pan over medium heat, pressing down firmly for a few seconds with a spatula and turning often until softened and fragrant.

In a saucepan, combine the chiles with water to cover, bring to a simmer over medium heat, and simmer for

5 minutes. Remove from the heat and let soak until very soft, about 10 minutes. Drain and tear into small pieces. In a blender, whirl the chiles, garlic, onion, orange juice, and beer until smooth. Pour into a small bowl and stir in $1/2$ tsp salt.

This salsa can be used right away, though it improves over time. Store in an airtight container in the refrigerator for up to 5 days.

ROASTED HABANERO CHILE & TOMATO SALSA

MAKES ABOUT 2 CUPS (16 FL OZ/500 ML)

4 tomatoes

1 small green bell pepper

1 habanero chile

3 tbsp canola oil

1 white onion, chopped

Kosher salt

Roast the tomatoes in a heavy frying pan over medium heat, turning as needed, until the skins are blistered and black in spots and the tomatoes begin to soften. Let cool slightly, then trim away the most blackened spots. Roast and peel the bell pepper and chile as directed on page 15. Remove the seeds and membranes from the bell pepper. Partially slit the chile on all 4 sides.

In a blender or food processor, whirl the tomatoes with their juice and the bell pepper until coarsely puréed. In a saucepan, warm the oil over medium heat, add the onion, and cook, stirring, until golden, about 3 minutes. Stir in the tomato mixture and cook until the sauce changes color, about 3 minutes. Add the chile, reduce the heat to medium-low, and simmer for about 15 minutes to blend the flavors.

Remove from the heat, remove and discard the chile, and stir in 1 tsp salt. Serve hot. To store, let cool, transfer to an airtight container, and store in the refrigerator for up to 5 days.

ÁRBOL & PASILLA CHILE SALSA

MAKES ABOUT 2 CUPS (16 FL OZ/500 ML)

4 árbol chiles, stemmed and seeded

2 pasilla chiles, stemmed and seeded

2 garlic cloves, unpeeled

6 tomatoes, coarsely chopped

Juice of $1/2$ lime

Kosher salt

Toast the chiles in a heavy frying pan over medium heat, pressing down firmly for a few seconds with a spatula and turning often, until softened and fragrant. In a saucepan, combine the chiles with water to cover, bring to a simmer over medium heat, and simmer for 5 minutes. Remove from the heat and let soak until very soft, about 10 minutes. Drain and tear into small pieces.

Roast the garlic cloves in the same frying pan over medium heat, turning them often, until they soften and their skins blacken, 8–10 minutes. Let cool, then peel.

In a blender or food processor, whirl the garlic, tomatoes, and lime juice just until broken up. Add the chiles and $1/2$ tsp salt and whirl to a slightly rough-textured consistency. If the mixture is too thick, add a little water as needed to thin. Store in an airtight container in the refrigerator for up to 5 days.

RED CHILE SAUCE

MAKES ABOUT 4 CUPS (32 FL OZ/1 L)

10 large guajillo chiles

1 tomato, chopped

4 garlic cloves

Kosher salt

2 tsp vegetable oil

3 tbsp finely minced white onion

Toast the chiles in a heavy frying pan over medium heat, pressing down firmly for a few seconds with a spatula and turning often, until softened and fragrant. In a saucepan, combine the chiles with water to cover, bring to a simmer over medium heat, and simmer for 5 minutes. Remove from the heat and let soak until very soft, about 10 minutes. Reserving the liquid in a separate bowl, drain the chiles, and tear into small pieces.

In a blender, whirl the chiles and their reserved soaking liquid, the tomato, garlic, and 1 tsp salt until a thick, smooth purée forms.

In a frying pan, warm the oil over medium heat. Add the onion and cook, stirring often, until just softened, 3–5 minutes. Pour the chile purée into the frying pan. Add ¼ cup (2 fl oz/60 ml) water to the blender, swirl to wash down the residue of the purée from the sides, and add to the pan. Heat the sauce, stirring constantly, until fragrant and slightly thickened, 3–5 minutes.

Transfer the sauce to a large measuring pitcher and add enough water to total 4 cups (32 fl oz/1 l) sauce, or thin to the desired consistency. Taste and adjust the seasoning with salt if needed. Store in an airtight container in the refrigerator for up to 5 days.

PICKLED JALAPEÑO CHILES

MAKES SIX ½-PT (8–FL OZ/250-ML) JARS

4 cups (32 fl oz/1 l) apple cider vinegar (5 percent acidity)
2 tbsp honey
Kosher salt
1 tbsp pickling spice
1 tbsp pink peppercorns
About 20 large or 30 small jalapeño chiles, stemmed and sliced ¼ inch (6 mm) thick

Have ready 6 hot sterilized ½-pt jars and their lids.

In a large nonreactive saucepan, combine the vinegar, honey, and 1 tsp salt and bring to a boil over medium-high heat.

Meanwhile, in each jar, put ½ tsp each pickling spice and pink peppercorns. Pack the jars tightly with the jalapeño slices to within ¾ inch (2 cm) of the rim.

Ladle the hot brine into the jars, leaving ½-inch (12-mm) headspace. Slide a metal chopstick or other thin tool down the side of each jar, between the glass and the chiles, a few times to release any air bubbles. Adjust the

headspace, if necessary, then wipe the rim of each jar clean and seal tightly with a lid.

Process the jars in a boiling-water bath for 7 minutes. Transfer the jars to a work surface, let sit undisturbed for 12 hours, then check for a good seal: press on the middle of each jar lid with a fingertip; if the lid springs up when you lift your finger, the seal failed. Store jars with a good seal in a cool, dark place for 2 weeks to mellow before using; they will keep for up to 1 year. Store jars with a failed seal in the refrigerator and use within 1 week.

SWEET & SMOKY BBQ RUB

MAKES ABOUT ⅔ CUP (5 OZ/155 G)

¼ cup (2 oz/60 g) granulated sugar
1 tbsp firmly packed brown sugar
¼ cup (1 oz/30 g) hot paprika
1 tbsp chipotle chile powder
1 tsp cayenne pepper
1 tsp smoked paprika
Kosher salt and freshly ground black pepper

In a small container, combine the sugars, paprika, chile powder, cayenne, smoked paprika, 1 tsp salt, and several grinds of black pepper. Cover tightly and shake vigorously to mix. Store in the pantry for up to 3 months.

SPICY DIJON MUSTARD

MAKES TWO ½-PT (8–FL OZ/250-ML) JARS

1⅓ cups (4 oz/125 g) dry mustard
2 cups (16 fl oz/500 ml) dry white wine or flat Champagne
1 yellow onion, chopped
3 garlic cloves, finely chopped
2 tsp sugar
Kosher salt

Have ready 2 hot sterilized ½-pt jars and their lids.

In a bowl, stir together the mustard and ½ cup (4 fl oz/125 ml) water until smooth. Set aside.

In a small nonreactive saucepan, combine the wine, onion, and garlic and bring to a boil over high heat.

Reduce the heat to medium, stir in the sugar and 2 tsp salt, and simmer, uncovered, stirring often, until reduced by half, about 20 minutes.

Pour the wine mixture through a fine-mesh sieve placed over the bowl holding the mustard. Stir to mix well. Transfer the mixture to the saucepan and cook over medium heat, stirring frequently, until thickened, about 20 minutes.

Spoon the hot mustard into the sterilized jars, leaving ¼-inch (6-mm) headspace. Slide a metal chopstick or other thin tool down the side of each jar, between the glass and the mustard, a few times to release any air bubbles. Adjust the headspace, if necessary, then wipe the rim of each jar clean and seal tightly with a lid. Store the jars in the refrigerator for at least 2 weeks before using. The mustard will keep for up to 1 year.

FRESH HORSERADISH SAUCE

MAKES ABOUT 1 CUP (8 OZ/250 G)

¼ cup (2 fl oz/60 ml) mayonnaise, preferably homemade

½ cup (4 oz/125 g) sour cream

3 tbsp grated fresh horseradish root

2 tbsp chopped fresh chives

1 tsp prepared yellow English mustard

1 tsp steak sauce or Worcestershire

In a small bowl, stir together the mayonnaise, sour cream, horseradish, chives, mustard, and steak sauce, mixing well.

The sauce can be used right away, though it tastes best if allowed to mellow for 1 day. Store in an airtight container in the refrigerator for up to 5 days.

CHILE-LEMON OIL

MAKES ONE 1-PINT (16–FL OZ/500-ML) BOTTLE

2 cups (16 fl oz/500 ml) extra-virgin olive oil

2 large lemons

3 or 4 dried whole chiles

1 bay leaf

Pour the olive oil into a small nonreactive saucepan. Working directly over the pan, grate the zest from the lemons, letting it fall into the oil. Add the chiles and bay leaf. Clip a candy thermometer onto the side of the pan. Heat the oil over medium-low heat until the thermometer registers 200°F (95°C). Cook at 200°F– 225°F (95°C–110°C) for 10 minutes. Let cool slightly.

Using a funnel, pour the oil into a bottle, discard the chiles and bay leaf, and cover tightly. Store in a cool, dark place for up to 1 month.

SPICY PEANUT SAUCE

MAKES ABOUT 1 CUP (8 OZ/250 G)

1 tbsp peanut oil

2 garlic cloves, minced

⅔ cup (5 fl oz/160 ml) chicken or vegetable broth

¼ cup (2 fl oz/60 ml) hoisin sauce

2 tbsp creamy peanut butter

1 tsp *each* Asian chile paste and tomato paste

½ tsp sugar

¼ cup (2 oz/60 g) finely chopped roasted peanuts

In a small saucepan, warm the oil over medium heat. Add the garlic and cook, stirring, for 1 minute. Whisk in the broth, hoisin sauce, peanut butter, chile paste, tomato paste, and sugar and bring to a simmer. Cook, stirring, for about 3 minutes to blend the flavors. Let cool to room temperature. Transfer the sauce to a serving bowl and sprinkle with the peanuts. Or store in an airtight container in the refrigerator for up to 5 days.

Index

weldon**owen**

1045 Sansome Street, Suite 100, San Francisco, CA 94111
www.weldonowen.com

Weldon Owen is a division of
BONNIER

WELDON OWEN, INC.

President & Publisher Roger Shaw
SVP, Sales & Marketing Amy Kaneko
Finance Manager Philip Paulick

Associate Publisher Jennifer Newens
Associate Editor Emma Rudolph

Creative Director Kelly Booth
Art Director Marisa Kwek
Senior Production Designer Rachel Lopez Metzger

Production Director Chris Hemesath
Associate Production Director Michelle Duggan

Director of Enterprise Systems Shawn Macey
Imaging Manager Don Hill

Photographer John Lee
Food Stylist Lillian Kang
Prop Stylist Glenn Jenkins

Make It Spicy

Conceived and produced by Weldon Owen, Inc.
Copyright © 2015 Weldon Owen, Inc.

Printed and bound by 1010 Printing, Ltd. in China

First printed in 2015
10 9 8 7 6 5 4 3 2

Library of Congress Cataloging-in-Publication
data is available.

ISBN 13: 978-1-61628-925-6
ISBN 10: 1-61628-925-2

ACKNOWLEDGMENTS
Weldon Owen wishes to thank the following people
for their generous support in producing this book:
Amanda Anselmino, Kristen Balloun, Stephen Lam,
Elizabeth Parson, and Sharon Silva.